## *A Shot at Redemption*
### or "Lucky, Lucky Me"

**by Bill Mahoney
as told to Don Morreale**

Copyright 2019 by Pickle Ball Press

ISBN 9781072962175

All rights reserved. No part of this book may be reproduced or transmitted in any form or by any means, electronic or mechanical, including photocopying, recording, or by any information storage and retrieval system, without permission in writing from the copyright owner.

This book was printed in the United States of America.

**Pickle Ball Press**
**Denver, Colorado**
www.donmorreale.com

*I believe that all memory is quantum, by which I mean that we only remember the past in little packets. Here is my life story as I remember it.*
*Bill Mahoney*
*Lakewood, Colorado, 2019*

# Table of Contents

1. A Brooklyn Boyhood – 1
2. New Paltz University – 9
3. Vietnam – 19
4. Re-entry and a Wedding – 30
5. Back to School – 35
6. Heading for Colorado – 41
7. The Gift Shop Caper – 47
8. Lori – 51
9. Adrienne and the Joker's Inn – 55
10. Mountain Rivers Detox – 58

*My Life in Pictures* – 65

11. Deer Haven – 82
12. The Real Estate Biz – 87
13. The Welcome-Home Viet Vets Parade – 91
14. A Baha'i Epiphany – 93
15. The Russia Adventure – 96
16. End of a Marriage. Rise of *Desert Rose* – 104
17. Taking Wing – 109
18. Kickin' Back in Florida – 115
19. Falling in Love with Joan – 117
20. Real Estate is Still in My Blood – 121
21. The Freedom Boating Club – 123
22. Travels – 125
23. Meeting My Son & Closing the Circle – 140

*Epilogue* – 146

## Chapter 1: A Brooklyn Boyhood

I grew up in Bay Ridge, Brooklyn, on 86th Street and Fort Hamilton Parkway. The Verrazano Bridge went right through the neighborhood. For awhile we were afraid they would take out our building to build the bridge, but in the end, they went just a block north of us.

We lived in a rent-controlled apartment building. I am not sure of the history of rent control, but it meant that we could live very cheaply. I think when my parents moved out in 1972 to retire to Florida like all good New Yorkers, they were still paying only $62.50 a month rent for the place.

While it was a small apartment – only three rooms – it was located in a safe neighborhood, which at the time meant a "white neighborhood." Who knows what it rents for now? It was probably only 500 to 600 square feet, with one bedroom, a tiny bathroom, a miniscule kitchen, a smallish living room, and a hallway that had to be used as living space.

We lived on the building's third floor. It wasn't a walk-up; there was an elevator, which was fun for us kids because we could play in it. It was small enough so that if you got your feet up off the floor and braced yourself against the sides, you could get it to stop in the middle of a trip. It was a rickety contraption, probably as old as the building, which I think was built sometime in the teens or '20s.

We were lower working class. My dad was a New York City fireman who joined the Department in 1937. This was before they unionized and started paying fireman a decent wage. So it was a steady job, but also a very low-paying one, which is why they had rent control for workers in New York. As for me, I thought the whole world was poor.

Actually, not really, because down towards the shore of Bay Ridge there were big mansions, so I knew there were rich people out there. I didn't consider us poor, exactly. We were working-class. Our neighborhood was both clean *and* run down. Again, I hate to put it in racial terms but it was a white neighborhood, so that meant it was a safe neighborhood.

Sixty-Ninth Street and Fifth Avenue – which was still Bay Ridge – was the "color line." That's what they called it, "the color line," and blacks and Puerto Ricans could not – and *did* not – live north of that line. Where we were, on 86th Street, was a large section of Brooklyn that was basically all white. We ran in nine gangs; the Italian and Irish gangs were sort of against the Scandinavian gangs (although there was some crossover), and everybody – Italians, Swedes, and Irish – was against the black and Puerto Rican gangs

One of my friends, a guy named Pendergast, had a skin condition called "chicken skin." So of course, we called him "Chicken Skin Pendergast," which was a very accurate description of the poor guy. There was another kid named Joey Legosso who was Italian and whom everybody liked. He could hit a Spaulding rubber ball a distance of three manhole covers, which was pretty rare.

But my absolute best friend growing up was a kid named Jackie Haber who lived around the corner from us on 85th St. He was also my best friend in college, mainly because he was a good alcoholic like I was. So we had that in common.

My parents were what I would call "Lace Curtain Irish." They were very concerned about how they and the family looked to the outside world, so everything had to be very proper. Basically, I lived two lives; one in my parents' house, and the other out on the street where I was free and could just be myself, i.e. wild and crazy. I'd go home and hide the stuff my dad didn't approve of – like my cigarettes – under the radiator out in the hallway, along with whatever money I had scammed because my parents didn't believe in giving us kids an allowance.

One of my early scams was selling firecrackers. There was this older kid in the neighborhood who we knew was dealing firecrackers, so two of us guys followed him on our bikes when he got on a bus that was headed towards Coney Island via 86th Street. When he got off, we followed him into a building and spied on him. When he left, we went up to the apartment he'd been in and knocked on the door. A big old Italian woman asked us what we wanted.

"We're here to buy some product," we said. I think she took pity on us two young Irish kids because she said, "Okay, you can come in." She pointed to a crippled guy sitting in the window looking down at 82$^{nd}$ Street, two floors below. "This here is Big Al," she said. Big Al was apparently the guy who took the orders for the firecrackers.

"You got money?" he said.

"Yeah, we got money," we replied.

"So whaddya want?" he said.

"We want three mats," which was…I forget how many little firecrackers in a mat…but the package included cherry bombs and 10 bottle rockets.

"That'll be $16," said Big Al. We handed over the money. "You're number 40. Be at the corner of 14$^{th}$ Avenue and 82$^{nd}$ Street at 8:00 o'clock tonight."

So we went there on our bikes and there were kids all down the block on *their* bikes, and at 8:00 o'clock a 1950 Chevy with darkened windows pulled up and a guy yelled out, "Forty!"

We rode our bikes up and he dumped our order out the window. There was no portion control or anything, although they were pretty accurate now that I think about it. So, anyway, we got those firecrackers and I was selling them to the other kids.

As I remember, this was when I was in the seventh grade. That was the year I got elected president of my class. The vice-president was a girl named Margaret Mary Duffy with whom I had an ongoing love/hate relationship.

The classrooms had these old desks that you could lift the lids up to store things in, so I smuggled the firecrackers into the classroom and stashed them in my desk. Margaret saw me hiding them and she got all uptight and ratted me out to the nuns.

They looked in the desk, found the firecrackers, ands naturally I got in trouble. I was impeached and Margaret took over as president of the class, which was fine with me…except for the fact that I lost the firecrackers, which was a blow, financially speaking.

I started this story by saying that I used to have to ditch all kinds of stuff outside the apartment before I went up to the third floor family apartment. Basically, I was leading two lives: my life out in the streets, and my home life, and yes I'm sure I got a beating or two along the way.

I had one brother, Gerald "Jerry" Mahoney, who was three-and-a-half years older than I was. We weren't really that close, not only because of the three-year difference in our ages, but also because we hung out in different crowds. Jerry hung out with a fairly straight crowd and I ran with a bunch of crazies.

My crowd were also alcoholics. When I was a Junior in High School, fifteen years old, I became a regular at a bar called the Coronet on Third Avenue and 83$^{rd}$ Street. I would sit at the bar and Irene, the owner/bartender, would serve me, no questions asked. I was there every afternoon drinking beer and anything else they happened to be serving. Eighteen was the legal drinking age, but I was a big kid. When I was 13, I was as tall as I am now (5'11" and shrinking). Irene would come over to me and she'd say, "Bill, you know I've got a young, young crowd in here, so if you know that anyone is not 18, please let me know. I could get in trouble for serving somebody under 18." And I'd say, "Sure. Sure. Okay, no problem." Of course, she didn't know that *I* was under 18 myself. Occasionally she'd even buy me a beer for helping her out.

Like a lot of alcoholics, I can remember very clearly my first real drink. Of course I'd had little sips of things here and there, but the year I turned 11 my parents took us out to Long Island to visit some old friends. The woman had been a nurse with my mother way back in the 1920s. It was New Year's Eve and their son and my brother and I were supposed to stay in the house while they went out. The kid next door, who was, I think, a year older than me, said, "Hey, I've got the key to my parents' liquor cabinet. It's New Year's Eve. Let's go have a drink!"

And so we did.

I don't remember what we drank, but we got roaring drunk. We went home and he went up to his bedroom on the second floor. By then it was probably around two in the morning. I started throwing rocks at his window and when he opened it up I said, "Let's keep going. Let's get back into your parents liquor cabinet!" He looked down at me and said, "You're crazy!" and slammed the window shut. He'd had enough, but as for me, I just wanted more – always more – which is why I believe I was born an alcoholic.

Now that I am 37 years sober, I firmly believe that alcoholism is a genetic disease. I hear that same story told over and over again in AA meetings; "I remember my first drink;" or "I found my best friend;" or "I always felt out of sorts as a kid growing up in Iowa and then I found booze." And then there's the second type, the three-martini lunch businessman, which is basically how AA got started back in 1935.

Anyway, when I was a kid there was no junior high school. In those days, you went from grammar school to high school. I went directly from a parochial grammar school – St. Anselm in Bay Ridge, Brooklyn – to St. Augustine High School which was in Park Slope, Brooklyn. I had to take either a 40-minute bus or train ride to get to school in Park Slope. St. Augustine was a very academic school and, of course, I grew up Catholic. My father was adamant about that. I mean as far as he was concerned, there was no such option as public school.

I've always considered myself as having a lazy brain. I've never studied in my life. I didn't have to. Things came easy to me. As a result, I was always getting into mischief and being sent to the principal's office where the good nuns would then call my father, and he'd come home from work and smack me upside the head for whatever it was I had done.

One time they called both my parents in for a meeting in which the nun apparently said, "I'm really frustrated. Maybe I shouldn't tell you this, but you know your son tested at the genius level. He should be getting straight A's. I don't know what his problem is."

Sometime after that, I again got into trouble, and that night my father came home and just threw up his hands and yelled, "You tested genius! Why? Why do you do these things?" So that's when I found out I was a genius. I think I tested out at an IQ of 164 or something. Maybe that's where my lazy brain came from. Maybe that's why life always seemed to come easy to me, and why I didn't have to study in school. I'd see other people studying, but I just didn't bother with it. And now I knew why.

So I think having such a high IQ shaped my life probably more than I realized. I was happy just barely getting through with C's and B's. St. Augustine High School was a very prestigious academic parochial school, so I knew that with a C or B average I could get into college when I graduated.

Getting into college was part of the immigrant's story I was living out. My grandparents came from Ireland sometime around the turn-of-the-century. I never knew when exactly, but sometime in the 1890s. My grandmother was a scrubwoman – she scrubbed the marble floors in the big buildings in Brooklyn and Manhattan – while my grandfather was a dockworker. And so what they told their kids was, "Get a steady job with benefits. Get a city job if possible." That was the next level up for an immigrant.

So the second-generation got city jobs; my father was a New York City fireman for 35 years, while my uncle was policemen. The third generation was supposed to get an education. The message was, "You can be better than we are. Get an education and you can hire people to do the heavy lifting. If your car goes bad, or your plumbing goes bad, you can pay someone to fix it. You won't have to work so hard if you get an education." So my only choice was to go to Catholic school and then on to college.

I applied to a bunch of colleges, but what I really wanted was to get into a state supported school, a public university. This was 1964 when the first of the baby boom generation, born in '46, were beginning to apply to college. So the colleges were all building like crazy because they knew this huge demographic was headed their way.

## Chapter 2: New Paltz University

I got a big thick book of colleges with statistics and little blurbs about what each of them offered. (This was before the Internet, so that's how you did it back then.) In the book, I found New Paltz University, which was part of the State University system. New Paltz University had been a state normal school before 1962, where they educated grammar school teachers. So it was mainly women who went there in those days. I think the ratio was four women for every man, and they had a dropout rate of only 2%, which suggested to me that it was probably a pretty easy school, academically speaking. "Now that's my kind of school!" I said to myself. "A lotta women and not too difficult."

By this time, I was more than ready to move out of our little three-room apartment and away from my lace-curtain parents with all of their rules and regulations. I was fighting a lot with my father because of all the restrictions. I couldn't stand restrictions – never could, never will – and so all of a sudden there I was, 90 miles upstate from New York City in a rural setting with mostly Jewish kids from Long Island in a state-supported school.  Somehow I got a scholarship to go there, so my parents were happy and so was I.  Finally, I was free of my parents.

  At New Paltz State University I was having the time of my life, totally out of control.  I was mainly hanging out with the townies because they were more partiers than anyone at the University.

  Because of all the Baby Boomers coming in, there was a lot of new construction going on around the campus.  We were packed in, three to a dorm room, because the campus was so overcrowded.  My two roommates were a kid from Brooklyn, Pat Frisina, and a guy from Long Island named Steve.

  We started hanging out with this guy named Noble Bright who was the University Registrar.  He was a gay man before it was okay to be gay.  His excuse for being gay was that he had been a registrar in Africa in his younger days, and since there were no women for sex, he became gay.  As I say, back in the '60s it was not yet acceptable to be gay, so a lot of gay men had backstories about why they were that way.  Anyway, Noble fell in love with my roommate Steve, so we started hanging out with him.  Steve was not gay but he was having a good time leading Noble on.

  This was also the start of drugs on campus.  The campus cops were straight out of the '50s.  They had no idea what was really going on.  Because we were hanging out with the locals, the police thought we were the connection between the drugs coming onto the campus and the locals who were supplying them.

  Pat Frisina, my roommate from Brooklyn, had a 1964 Corvair we'd ride around in, and so the campus police started following us. Noble Bright, who was a rebel to begin with, knew how ridiculous it was that the cops thought the drugs were coming onto campus through us. So he said, "Borrow my Mercedes and you can split up and that will confuse them."

I was taking all social studies courses because we didn't have to do anything but go to the talks and write a few papers. Steve and I were taking the same courses, so when we had a paper due, I would start opening books on the topic and just write as fast as I could. Meanwhile, Steve was a good typist, so when I was finished I'd give him the handwritten copy and he would start typing. I would read to where he left off and continue writing to finish his paper. I never went back and did a second draft of anything. We were getting B's and C's, which was good enough for both of us.

The other thing that happened while I was at school that first year was that I got a girl pregnant. As I mentioned earlier, I came from an Irish/Italian neighborhood where everybody was Catholic. I had gone to an all-boys Catholic high school, and after school we would meet the girls from the Catholic all-girls high school at the neighborhood soda fountain. Good Catholic girls all talked about doing "it" – the big "it" – but of course, none of them ever really did "it." Being a good Catholic boy, it never even occurred to me that girls might actually want to do it. Needless to say, when I went to college, I was still a virgin.

There were a lot of Jewish girls from Long Island at New Paltz, and I discovered that Jewish girls from Long Island didn't just talk about it, they *did* it. That having been said, the woman I finally got around to doing it with was not Jewish. She was Irish, although she'd been adopted by a German family who gave her the name Lucille.

Lucille and I started having rollicking teenage sex in the backseat of a red '53 Buick convertible that was parked in back of a bar in New Paltz. Couples in the bar would take turns steaming up the windows and making a mess on the seats.

The boys in the dorms were totally free to come and go as they pleased, but the girls had a curfew. They had to sign out when they left, and sign in when they returned, and there were dorm mothers who made sure they complied.

As an aside here, my wife to be (not the girl I got pregnant) signed out one evening and we spent the night in the back seat of the car freezing our asses off. She wasn't much of a drinker so I don't know how drunk she may have been, but when she failed to sign back in that night, she got suspended for the rest of the quarter.

I was just out of Brooklyn and still a virgin, as was Lucille, and somehow we ended up going to bed together (or rather, "backseat together") and within the first couple of weeks after our "inaugural ball," she started missing her period.

My first reaction when she told me was, "God got me." Which sounds crazy to me now, but I had been inculcated with twelve years of Catholic School guilt, and what better divine punishment than to be zapped by God for having sex with the first girl you'd ever been to bed with?

Lucille and I talked about going to Poughkeepsie to get an abortion, which was totally illegal in those days. This meant we would have had to find a doctor willing to do it under the table. Lucille, however, was a good Catholic girl and a good person, so instead of terminating the pregnancy, she went ahead and told her parents. Naturally, her parents freaked out and called my parents who were surprisingly sanguine about the whole affair. It was one of the few times when my father actually stood by me.

Lucille's father had a successful real estate business in New Jersey. He took me aside and said, "Listen, if you marry my daughter, I'll set you up in business. I'll even buy you a house."

I talked it over with my dad. "I really want to finish college," I told him. "I'm not ready to be married." I expected him to say, "Son, you're going to take care of this girl, and that's that." Instead he said, "It's your life, and I'll back you up, whatever you decide to do. If you don't want to marry her, that's your decision."

In the end, Lucille went to a Catholic home for unwed mothers on the East Side of Manhattan overlooking the East River. I would go and visit her whenever I was in town. On one visit, I went to the home, knocked on the door, and one of the nuns opened it a crack to see who it was. "Lucille's not here," she said, and slammed the door. As I was walking away, one of the pregnant girls came running out and said, "Lucille has gone into labor. She's at the hospital in Midtown."

So I went up there to see her and our new baby. Even though I was the father, since we weren't married I had no rights to see either of them. That's the way it was back then. To get around that little technicality, I just said, "I'm here to see the Lugar baby (appropriating her last name, which was Lugar).

A nurse pointed me in the direction of a room full of newborns in bassinets and said, "That one is the Lugar baby." So I got to see my son. I didn't see Lucille, however. I don't remember if she did not want to have contact with me or if I just blew it off, but that was the last time I would see my son for the next 52 years.

I went back to New Paltz and resumed my studies. Right across the Pennsylvania State line there was this place called Reedman Motors, which claimed to be the largest used car dealer in the world, carrying every new car on the market except for Cadillacs. This was where all good New Yorkers went to buy their cars. They had a whole section of used cars for under $100. They also had a test track where you could try them out. For another three dollars, you could get a 30-day temporary Pennsylvania tag. I bought a '55 Plymouth station wagon for $39.00 that seemed to run pretty good. I also got the $3.00 temporary tags, and drove it back to New Paltz.

When I got back to campus, the dormitory was empty and I thought, "Well this is boring," so I drove into town looking to see what kind of trouble I could get into. Cruising around, I noticed that there was this gas station that had a lot where they sold Christmas trees. It was late, they were closed, and there didn't seem to be any security around to guard it. So, naturally, I pulled in and began stuffing Christmas trees into the back of the Plymouth. I was so drunk that I didn't see the police car behind me, and as soon as I drove off the lot, he pulled me over.

He took me to see a judge. After-hours in New Paltz the court was closed, so at night, the judge would hold hearings on his back porch. The cop called him on our way to his house. "Sam," he said, "I got somebody for ya. I'm bringin' him in."

As it happened, I'd already met this judge. His nickname was "*The-Longer-The-Hair-The-Longer-The-Sentence-Schneider.*" I'd appeared before him previously on a drunk-and-disorderly charge for peeing on the yellow line down the middle of the street.

Actually, now that I think of it, this was the third weekend in a row I'd had to appear before him. It was always a $20 fine and a warning, and I'd fork over the $20 and that would be it. This time the charge was theft of a two-dollar Christmas tree, so I was waiting for him to fine me and let me go. Instead he said "That'll be 30 days in the county jail." There was nobody at the University I could call to come and tell the judge some bullshit like my mother had died, so I had to do the time. I was in jail for the finals and flunked out of school.

When I got out of jail, I hooked up with some local townies and got drunk over the Christmas holiday. One night there were like five or six of us just sprawled out in this big room, drunk on our asses, and in walks my father. Somehow, he'd tracked me down. My dad was a formidable man when he was angry. He was, I could see, more than a little put out with me. "Come on!" he barked. "Let's go!"

We spent the whole trip back to Brooklyn in stony silence. I moved back into the apartment, which lasted for about three weeks, tops. I would go out and get drunk every night. Then I'd came stumbling in, trying to be as quiet as possible getting into bed, which was in the same bedroom where my parents slept. I was used to getting drunk and sneaking into bed. I'd figured out very early in my drinking career, like at age 13 or 14 or 15, that if I drank, let's say, six beers, I would lay down and the room would spin around, but if I drank 15 beers I would just pass out. So I'd come in, totally plastered, right after my parents went to bed and I'd pass out and not worry about it.

My parents were, of course, aware of how out-of-control I was. But they did not know how to sit me down and say, "Listen son, you're out of control and this can't go on." So nothing was ever said.

One morning around 2:00 AM, I rolled in and stumbled over something just inside the door. I turned the lights on and there were two suitcases, all packed and ready to go. So I took the hint and left and spent the rest of the night riding back and forth on the subway. I wasn't feeling anything in particular. I was too drunk to feel anything.

The next morning, I called some friends and learned that a friend-of-a-friend had an apartment on W. 73rd St. in Manhattan and was looking for a roommate. The apartment was really just the front room in a brownstone that had been broken up into two apartments. I shared it with a guy whom we called Lurch. We called him that because he was this big tall guy who had gotten into a motorcycle accident and planted his face in the asphalt. So he looked like Lurch from the Adams Family TV show. Lurch put me up there and not long after that he moved out, leaving the place to me. The rent was $26 a week. I got a couple friends to move in with me and got a job at a firm called Anglo Fabrics down at 39th St. and Sixth Avenue, in the Garment District not far from Times Square.

I was earning about $60 a week, which was just above minimum wage. Rolls of fabric would come in, and my job was to cut a little piece off the roll and staple it into a book and write down the number of the sample.

When buyers came in, they would look at the swatch and tell me to go and fetch roll number 62424 or whatever. As hung over as I usually was, I always managed to get the numbers right. I guess they had had people who couldn't even do that much.

Where I lived was a couple of miles away from where I worked. The subway at the time cost 15 cents, which was also the price of a beer at the neighborhood bars. Payday was Friday, so I would drink through the weekend while simultaneously trying to save enough to be able to take the subway to work and back during the week. However, if it came down to a choice between buying a beer and saving enough to take the subway, the beer always won out.

There were weeks when I didn't have the money for the subway, so I would walk the 34 blocks south to work in the mornings, and an equal number of blocks north to get home. My walk took me past Lincoln Center, which was at 62nd St. There were all kinds of buskers performing in the big square in front of Lincoln Center, so it was a great time to walk by and stop and check out the action.

On days when I *did* have enough to take the subway to and from work, I'd get off at 72nd Street, which was a big subway stop. I'd climb the stairs and emerge right in the middle of Amsterdam and Columbus, which were big, wide avenues. Between those two streets was a long thin park where all the junkies used to hang out. It was popularly known as Needle Park and I'd have to walk past the junkies and then cross the street to get to 73rd where I lived.

Close to my stop was a doughnut shop where some of the most beautiful men I'd ever seen used to congregate. They were gay guys, some of them in drag.

I'd walk by and say hi and get my butt pinched, and just laugh.

On the corner of 73$^{rd}$ and Columbus Avenue, there was an apartment building where, in the summer, all the windows would be open. I'd hear opera coming out of one apartment, and the music of a grand piano coming out of another. The building was filled with performers.

When I had to walk home, I'd go through a black neighborhood, then a Puerto Rican neighborhood, followed by an Italian neighborhood, and finally the Irish neighborhood. On the corner of Seventh Avenue, there was a Chinese section with a laundry. So walking home was like walking through the world, which was always a treat for me.

After three or four months at Anglo Fabrics, I got down to working just Tuesdays, Wednesdays, and Thursdays, mainly because I would be too drunk after the weekend to come in on Mondays, and since Friday was the last day of the week, I would skip work to get a head start on my drinking.

I was certain I'd get fired but instead, Fred Brown, who was the manager of the place, called me into his office and said, "You know, I really like you, Bill. I know this job is beneath you and that's why you've been skipping work lately. So we're going to give you a promotion and a raise. We're re-vamping our system and as soon as we figure out what we're doing, you'll have some new duties. So in the meantime, here's a desk. Just come in every day and sit here."

My kind of job. I worked there for about nine months and it was a nice life…wild and free. Or so I thought…

## Chapter 3: Vietnam

It was January 1966, and the Vietnam War was raging. I had flunked out of college with a zero grade-point average because, being in jail, I hadn't been able to take the exams. In the past, I could go to the professors and say, "Jeez, I'm so sorry," and somehow talk my way into a C or D. It was at least a grade, which was enough to allow me to stay in college. But having flunked out, I no longer had a student deferment, and so now I was a prime target for the draft.

After I'd worked at Anglo for about nine months, sure enough I got my draft notice. It was September 1966 and this was the largest draft call America had ever seen. The Gulf of Tonkin had just happened and Secretary of Defense McNamara, with a scowl on his face and hate in his eyes, appeared on the front page of the New York Times talking about how horrible these people were for shelling our little boat in the Gulf of Tonkin. General Westmoreland backed him up by saying we would need another 200,000 troops to win the war in Vietnam. It was a very unpopular war, so they had to manufacture this bullshit to galvanize the country. When I saw that article in the Times, I knew the jig was up.

    I agonized over whether I should run away to Canada, or maybe see if I could get a medical deferment. As a kid, I'd broken my arm at the elbow and I still had a bump on it. It was well known in the drunken kid community that there were doctors out there who would sign papers for 50 bucks. So I thought, "I'll get a doctor's note saying that this arm is very weak and maybe that will get me out." I got a phony doctor's note saying that I had a bad back and that I had broken my arm as a kid and it had healed a little crooked in the elbow.

    I was also hoping that maybe all of the drunk and disorderly charges might get me out of it for being morally unfit to serve. I went up to New Paltz and got the records of the four or five drunk-and-disorderlies I'd been charged with, plus the 30 days I'd spent in the clink for theft, and went back to Brooklyn hoping against hope that I could bullshit my way out of having to go to Vietnam.

    I went to the draft board for my physical and did the old Arlo Guthrie routine. "You don't want me. I'm a criminal. Here's my criminal record: drunk and disorderlies, plus I have physical problems. Here's the letters from my doctors."

    I went down the line seeing each doctor, and at the end some guy said, "You're just the kind of man we need, son. You're exactly what we're looking for. Here's your orders." At that point, my choices were either to go into the military, or disappear and be a fugitive. I didn't have the nerve to run away to Canada, so I decided to just go ahead and report for duty. When it was time to leave, I went to say goodbye to my folks. I could see how much my father was in favor of my going into the service. "It'll make a man out of you," he said, clapping me on the shoulder.

So in September of 1966, I and a whole bunch of other local boys reported for duty at the draft hall in Brooklyn. From there, we were transported by train down to Fort Jackson, South Carolina, all of us scared shitless. As soon as we got there, they did exactly what we have all seen in the movies and on television. They started yelling and screaming at us, getting right up in our faces and trying to scare the hell out of us. We were tough kids from Brooklyn, so we didn't scare easily, but they definitely put the fear of God into us. They issued us uniforms, buzz cut our hippy hair (that hurt), and put us into barracks.

There were these four guys in my basic training group who really should not have been there. One of them, named Pakdikian, was just a roll of blubber, like 300 pounds of pure flab and not a muscle in his body. The second guy, who was around six-foot-six, wore size 16 shoes, weighed in at 120 lbs, and was totally uncoordinated. The third guy was tiny – I'd say under five feet tall. The fourth guy's trick was that he could throw up on cue, which he did, frequently and copiously, barfing on the desk of any officer he happened to come before. None of this had mattered to the guys at the draft board. This was the largest draft call in the history of the country, after all, and they needed bodies. So everybody passed. I guess they figured, "Get 'em in, and we'll filter 'em out later in boot camp."

During basic training, these four guys got together and formed their own little four-man "F

Troop." We'd be lined up and the drill sergeant would yell, "Left face!!" and the four of them would all turn right. And when they ordered us to start running, they would trip over each other and fall down on purpose. In an effort to shame and embarrass them, the drill instructors put them in their own separate tent across from the barracks...which didn't matter to us. We loved these guys. If they gave them extra duty, forcing them to miss a meal, we'd sneak extra food to them. The Army kept them through all eight weeks of basic training and put them through hell before finally letting them go.

The first 5 mile run we took – and we took a lot of them, – I would see people dropping out or falling down, they were so out of shape. As was I. I was wheezing and dying to just give up like those other guys. Then I saw this truck following the unit and picking them up and I said, "That's for me." So I fell down and they picked me up and we rode the rest of the way behind the poor guys who were still running. Nobody said a word to us, just took our names and that was it. Or so we thought.

That night they served us a big dinner in the mess hall, after which they called those of us who'd dropped out and said, "Now you guys are going to run again." Then they ran us and ran us and ran us 'til well past midnight. If you stopped they would just get right in your face; "Come on soldier. Move it! Move it! Move it!"

Whenever somebody fell down, they made us run in a circle around them until they got up. When we couldn't run anymore, they took us to an area where we had to low-crawl under barbed wire, as if we were under fire. By midnight, we were all puking and hallucinating.

It was tough, but I learned something that night; never be first and never be last. "Don't ever drop out again," I said to myself. "If everyone else can do it, *you* can do it." It was a lesson that has served me well throughout the rest of my life.

After four weeks of basic training, we were given some time off. Sue, the girl I had dated in college after knocking up Lucille, drove down from New York in a 1960 Ford Falcon for a little visit. We stayed in a cheap motel off base. I had concentrated hard and shot "*Expert*" on the rifle range because I knew if I shot well I could get a three-day pass.

Sue was taken aback at first by the new look – me with a bald head – but she knew that was what the Army did to guys. So for the next three days, we did what young couples do; we fucked, then talked, then fucked, then talked some more. After that, I went back to base for the last four weeks of training.

In addition to the intense physical training we got in basic, they gave us tests to see what we were good at, and then – this being the Army – they put us in exactly the opposite thing. As for me, I'm lost when it comes to high tech, so naturally they sent me to Fort Gordon, Georgia, for an eleven-week course in how to be a radio teletype operator.

Then I was given a job in the finance department at Fort Gordon, while everybody else was being shipped off to Vietnam. I breathed a sigh of relief, thinking the job would keep me in the US and out of harm's way.

The harsh training in basic didn't sweat the alcoholic out of me, and at Fort Gordon, I learned all about the joys of White Lightning. I also started hanging out with the black guys. That was because the white guys had no class at all. They were mainly a bunch of southern crackers while the black guys were cool.

So we would go to these honky-tonks out in the country and drink White Lightning out of Mason jars. And that's how I got into the trouble that eventually led to my being kicked into Vietnam.

After basic training, they gave us leave to go home for a week or two. While I was back, I went to Reedman Motors, where I found a 1960 Chevy 283 for around $200 and drove it back down to Georgia where I became a hotshot because nobody else on base had a car.

I got into some kind of trouble and was placed on restriction, which meant I was confined to base. But I had this car and I was itching to go someplace and get drunk, so I snuck off base one night, got drunk, and on the way back I forgot that the brakes were mushy. If you wanted to stop the car, you had to pump the hell out of them.

I came up to a red light and ran smack into the back of a major who was out with his girlfriend. Naturally, he was pissed and wanted me court-martialed, or at a minimum given an Article 15, which is a lesser charge where you just get broken down in rank and pay.

So my CO said, "We'll give you an Article 15, bust you down to E-1 (which is below Private) and fine you half your pay for the next three to six months"

This did not, unfortunately, satisfy the Major. He pulled some strings and cut orders for me to go to Vietnam. Because I worked in finance, I had access to my records. This was before computers and your records were kept in a file in a locked drawer. I had the key, so I got my file out and removed the Article 15 from my records.

Within a week, I was on a plane to Vietnam, and when I got there, they promoted me to E-4 (Corporal) because they didn't know about the Article 15. It never did catch up with me and I kept my normal pay.

I was sent directly to Camp Benjamin, a point camp just outside of Pleiku. It was pretty primitive, as was the equipment they gave me to use. I had been trained at Fort Gordon as an *05C20* – a radio teletype operator – so I thought maybe I would get a job in an office with big radio teletype equipment. Instead, I had to go into the jungle on patrol, carrying a huge pack full of communication gear on my back. This made me a prime target for the VC, who understood that if they could disrupt communications, they could attack at will. Needless to say, I was not happy.

Camp Benjamin housed the mechanics whose job it was to keep the helicopters flying, and the warrant officers whose job it was to fly them. I got there just before the Tet ceasefire and would work 12-hours-on/12-hours-off, from 6:00 at night to 6:00 in the morning. We were the communication center for the people on the perimeter as well as for the Huey's in the air.

One morning during the Tet New Year ceasefire, just as the sun was coming up, a Huey pilot called in and said, "Hey, there's this bunch of guys on the road into Pleiku."

I radioed back, "Yeah? So?"

"I don't think these guys are just New Year's revelers. I counted 43 of them and they appear to be armed. I think they're VC. What should I do?" Since the ceasefire was on, we weren't supposed to fire on them.

"I don't know," I radioed back. "I'll send somebody to get an officer to advise us." As it happened, we could not find an officer. I called this into the pilot who radioed back, "I think these guys are going to try and take Pleiku."

"Well then, do what you have to do," I told him. On his own initiative, he strafed them with his 50-caliber machine gun. I don't know how many he killed. There was a big inquiry afterward because we had broken the ceasefire. The North claimed that we had shot up what was just a military parade. I was exonerated at the inquiry, but I like to tell people that I was the one who broke the Tet Cease-Fire.

Our platoon sergeant had gotten himself killed in an ambush, and the "powers that be" got together and decided I should take his place. I wasn't particularly happy about it; more responsibility meant more risk. As it happened, fate intervened.

Earlier in my tour of duty, I had written to my gay friend, Nobel Bright, the Registrar at New Paltz, telling him I had flunked out and was now in Vietnam. "I would very much like to come back to University," I wrote, "Any chance you could help me out?" Nobel pulled some strings and just before I was to be promoted, I got a letter admitting me back into New Paltz. At that time, if you had a letter stating that you had been admitted to a four-year academic college, you could get a 90-day early out. So instead of having five or six months left in Vietnam, I now only had two months left to go, so I was passed over for the promotion and got sent instead to Cam Ranh Bay, which was a huge Air Force base in a secure area of the country. I honestly believe Noble's letter saved my life.

Technically speaking, I was now out of the war. I had two months to kill with nothing to do, so I got a job running the recreation center. This meant I could spend my days hustling pool. I made friends with this huge black guy who was maybe not the brightest bulb on the tree, and together we did our best to get into mischief.

We lived in tents surrounded by sand bags three or four feet high, so if you got incoming with shrapnel you could get behind the sandbags. Everybody hid their stashes of marijuana and other drugs in the sandbags. We knew where the drugs were, so we thought it would be funny to go and pick up everybody's stash, bring it to the rec center, dump it all out onto the ping-pong table, and then invite everybody to come and retrieve their stashes.

While we thought this was hilarious, the victims of our little prank failed to see the humor. Fortunately, my friend was so big and strong that there was no physical retaliation. There were a lot of threats, however. But since everybody could come and get their drugs back, none of it went anywhere.

Most of the guys on the base were lifers, mainly southern crackers, and they would pick on my black buddy mercilessly, giving him extra duty filling sandbags and moving furniture. This was clearly a case of discrimination, so he decided to file a complaint with the IG (Inspector General) who was supposed to investigate such things.

The problem was that the Inspector General's Office was only open from 9:00 to 5:00. The crackers knew he wanted to file a complaint, so whenever he had a little time off, they would give him extra duty so he wouldn't be able to get to the IG's office in time.

Finally, he got so frustrated that he strapped a couple of grenade belts across his chest, and planted himself in front of a large cache of fuel tanks. When the OD (Officer of the Day) walked by he pulled the pin on a grenade and said, "If I don't see a general here in the next hour, I'm gonna blow this motherfucker up." There were hundreds of thousands of gallons of fuel in those tanks and if he threw the grenade, the whole camp would get blown to hell.

So the OD went running to try and find a general…which he never did, although he did manage to find a full bird colonel to come and talk my friend down. "Okay son," said the colonel, "We understand the stress you're under, so we're going to let you go. You'll be on a plane day after tomorrow and you can go home. So just put the pin back in and get on with your life."

My sergeant, who knew that me and the black guy were friends, hated me and I hated him. He was a southern cracker and he had put me on extra duty filling sandbags when I had the flu. I'd even been to the doctor, which didn't matter in the least to him. He still slammed me with extra duty.

So I wrote him up for an Article 15, a disciplinary procedure for minor offenses. But he was a lifer and getting this on his record would hurt his chances for advancement. So he had retaliated by putting *me* up for an Article 15. I couldn't care less. I was short. I was going home soon and I didn't give a rat's ass. But an Article 15 on his record would be serious for him and I knew it.

So he went to the company commander and said, "Listen. Mahoney is being a pain in the ass, so if you would cut his orders now he will be out of all our hair." By that time, I only had two or three weeks left, just enough time to nail the sergeant, so the Commanding Officer cut the orders and the next day I was on the plane going home with my buddy, both of us with an honorable discharge.

In Vietnam, everybody smoked pot on a daily basis – very strong pot. I really thought I was addicted to it. I smoked it every day, dawn to dusk. I wanted to bring some back with me but the Army had put the fear of god into us about smuggling drugs. They even showed us a film about it. The message was clear; "Don't try to smuggle anything through customs. They're professionals and they will catch you and put you in jail." I'll admit, they had me scared, but I went ahead and did it anyway

I figured the best way to sneak it into the "world" would be to get these Mennen Foot Powder plastic containers, dump out the contents and stuff them full of pot. Filled with marijuana, they were the same weight as the powder. I filled six giant Mennen Foot Powder bottles with pot, put a little piece of plastic over the contents, and dumped in a half inch or so of the foot powder in case the inspectors got nosey and opened them up. As it happened, nobody even gave me a second look. The customs agents were not army and they did not want to bust a Vietnam veteran coming home from the war. So we breezed through customs, and I arrived back in the US with a shitload of pot.

## Chapter 4: Re-entry and a Wedding

With a week to kill before I was to be mustered out, I was sent to Fort Louis, Washington where, first order of business, I went downtown to get a drink. I walked into a bar and the first thing I saw were naked women dancing in cages. I was shocked. Not only that, by the time I got back to college in 1968, the dorms were all coed. The world had changed in the two years since I'd gone into the Army.

Two weeks after I got back from Vietnam, Sue and I got married. She was the second woman I ever went to bed with. Before I left for Vietnam, I told my friends, "This is my fiancé, so take care of her for me."

While I was in Nam, Sue had been my lifeline to the world. She would send me cassette tapes telling me what was going on back home. I had introduced her to my parents, so on the tapes she'd give me a report on how they were doing. Unlike me and my friends, Sue was not a drinker. She lived in Jackson Heights in Queens, and she had a car. My drunken friends would call her, and she'd drive over to Brooklyn and be the designated driver. Through her, I was able to keep in touch with all of them as well.

They loved her and watched out for her while old Bill was off fighting the war. On the last cassette I sent to her I said, "Sue, when I get back, we might as well just get married." That was how I proposed to her. We set the date for June 15$^{th}$, exactly two weeks after my return.

I would be marrying into a good family. Sue's mother was a wonderful woman. Her name was Josephine. She was Jewish, born in Czechoslovakia. When the Nazis invaded, she had managed to escape to Sweden, where she hid out until they caught her and sent her to Bergen-Belsen death camp. She was 18 years old.

One day, standing in line for the daily ration of soup and a piece of bread, somebody said "Tell them you're a nurse." She went to the guy in charge and made the claim. She was assigned to the prison hospital. There was no medicine to give the patients, and when they died, she would prop them up in their beds. So when the unsuspecting Nazis did their daily headcounts, they would count the dead as well as the living, and the women on the ward would get their rations. That little trick kept them from starving, and that was how Josephine made it through the war.

At the time the Nazis invaded, her fiancé joined the Czech Army, which didn't last too long. Instead of allowing himself to be drafted into the German Army, he got into the Czech Merchant Marines and ended up in America. When he got off the boat, the immigration guys said, "Welcome to America. Here's your uniform." He fought the war in the American Army.

After the war, he went in search of Josephine. Because he was an American soldier, the Red Cross helped him search for her. He finally found her in a Soviet relocation camp and got her out. He married her right away and brought her to New York, where nine months later Sue, my wife-to-be, was born. When she was born, her mother and father, who had just come out of Nazi Germany and who had no idea what America was all about, had had her baptized. They had also changed their last name from Reisman to Reed.

    Although she was in fact Jewish, she agreed to marry me in the Catholic Church. This was due to my hubris, and it was totally unfair to her and her family, but that's what we did. We were married for three years, but got divorced when I decided to move to Colorado.

    I lost track of Sue and didn't hear from her again for the next 45 years, around the time I decided to marry my current wife, Joan. Joan was a good Catholic girl, and she wanted us to have a Catholic wedding, which meant I would have to get a formal annulment signed by the Church.

    I got in touch with Sue through the registrar at New Paltz University. They took my email address, forwarded it to Sue, who emailed me back. She was now going by the name "Suska," and had re-embraced her Jewish heritage.

    As it turns out, she's had a good life. She had three children and is living in Portland, Maine with the guy she married after me. "We haven't made a lot of money, but we've had a good life," she told me. It was nice to get in touch with her and get caught up.

    The night before I'd married her, all my good drunken Irish and Italian friends had put on a bachelor party for me at somebody's apartment in a residential section of Brooklyn down by Shore Road. I broke out the marijuana I had brought back from Vietnam. This weed was more powerful than anything these guys had ever tried and everyone got really stoned, as well as drunk.

By the time 3:00 AM rolled around, I was passed out cold. Somebody nudged me awake and said, "Let's go to the bar and see if we can make *Last Call*," which made perfect sense to me. The problem was that the bars were all on Third Avenue, which was an uphill climb five or six blocks from the apartment. I was the only one with a car, so I got behind the wheel and drove, and ended up smashing into a parked car. I lost two bottom teeth in the accident, and my two friends got huge gashes that would require stitches. So we got out of the car and walked the remaining distance to the bar, where we got some rags to staunch the blood.

The bartender gave us a drink and told us to get the hell out of there. We bled all over the cab on the way to the hospital where the cops finally caught up with us. In the Emergency Room, they pulled the remainder of the tooth that had broken off in the accident – which I did not feel because I was so drunk and stoned – and were now sewing up the gashes on the foreheads of my two friends.

The cop who was taking my statement was a good Irishman. "So tell me what happened," he said.

"A parked car jumped right out in front of me," I explained, still thinking this was all a big joke.

"No, no, no," he replied. "I cannot write that down. Tell me, were there any cats around?"

Catching his drift, I said, "Oh yeah. A cat ran out across the road and I swerved to miss him and I hit this park car."

"Okay," he said, "that I can put in my report." It also didn't hurt that I mentioned to him that my father was a New York City fireman, and my uncle a New York City policeman. I also mentioned *his* name of course. The officer, being a good Irishman, never acknowledged what I'd told him. He just said, "I'll write it up and we'll see what happens. Have a good time at your wedding." I never heard anything more about the incident. For all I know, the cop may have just torn up the report.

To make matters worse, it had been Sue's mother's car I'd been driving. I'm sure she had insurance on it, so the damage was paid for by the insurance company. I never heard another word about it. As usual, I was skating through life.

The next day we got married at my Brooklyn parish, Saint Anselm's, which was this big new marble church in the neighborhood. Over 200 people were there: her good Jewish family and my good Catholic family and all the guys that had been at the bachelor party, who were still pretty hung over.

As a wedding present, somebody paid for our wedding night in the honeymoon suite at the Waldorf-Astoria Hotel in Manhattan, where I proceeded to climb on top of my new wife and promptly pass out. Sue, being the good, forgiving Al-Anon that she was, did not even get mad. The next day we went to St. Thomas, Virgin Islands and stayed at Charlotte Amalie for a week's honeymoon.

## Chapter 5: Back to School

After the honeymoon, we moved back up to New Paltz. Sue had already graduated and was teaching in Walden, New York. We rented an apartment on the first floor of a new house built by a guy who had bought the land from a retired mafia enforcer from New York named "Strawberry Joe." Joe's trick was to take a vial of acid, walk by his victim and throw it in his face, leaving an ugly red scar that resembled a strawberry. Ergo, the nickname.

Our landlord wanted to sell us a piece of the property, so I talked to my brother Jerry and we decided to buy 12 acres from him if he would build us a pond that we could stock with fish. Our land was right below a pond that had been dug and stocked with largemouth bass by Strawberry Joe. The landlord agreed to build the pond and eventually small fish started swimming into it through the piping that had been laid in to feed it. We kept that chunk of ground for years, thinking maybe we would build a house on it. That never happened. Years later, we sold it and made a profit.

Meanwhile, I was taking more than a full load of credits. I had about 2 ½ years left to finish my degree, but I wanted to finish it in two. Somehow I managed to maintain an astoundingly good grade point average without doing a whole lot of work.

The reason I was getting such good grades my second time around was that I had the system figured, and now I knew how to work it. I wore tweed jackets with leather patches on the elbows and smoked a pipe. I wore my hair short while everybody else's was down to their shoulders. I seemed serious, while all my classmates wanted to do was protest and burn buildings down.

This was 1968, '69, and all the state universities were expanding like crazy to accommodate the Baby Boomers. There were a lot of professors teaching at New Paltz with newly minted PhD's. One of them was a Dr. Jerry Benjamin, who taught political science. He was a good Jewish boy who'd just received his PhD from one of the city universities. He'd had his nose in the books for the whole time that Vietnam was happening, so he didn't know much about what was going on. Everybody except me had long hair and was disrespectful and just wanted to have a good time. Nobody really wanted an education.

With my short hair, my pipe and my tweed jacket, a married man living in a house instead of a commune, I looked like an island of sanity in the middle of all this chaos. Professor Benjamin would often ask me to explain to him what was happening, and I would tell him to the best of my ability.

He and I became good friends. I ended up taking four courses from him, and I got A's in three of them without having to do any work. The last one, he gave me a B, saying, "Bill, you haven't done anything this semester. Nothing. So I've got to give you a B." He seemed really distraught about it.

To be honest, I hadn't done anything for the other three courses either, but these were political science courses and so there wasn't much to do but BS…which was why I could get through them without doing a whole lot of work.

Despite my outward appearance of clean cut sobriety, I was still drinking pretty heavily. I had no idea yet that alcoholism was a disease, but I did know that once I took a drink, that was it. I would drink for the rest of the day, and nothing else mattered. So I decided to devote every *other* day to my husbandly duties and schoolwork, and the days in between to serious drinking. This would be my pattern for the next two years.

On my drinking days, I would get very drunk, black out, and not remember driving home. On my sober days, my wife and I would have sex, and I would do what little studying I needed to do. I told myself that this was a good solution for me because it meant that at least I wasn't drunk *all* the time. As far as I was concerned, life was working out just fine.

One of my professors pulled me aside one day and said "Mahoney, you're a good Irishman. You should go and get a Masters Degree from Cornell and start working for the unions. I know people at Cornell in the School of Industrial and Labor Relations. I'll get in touch with them and get you in." This made sense to me, but I had some concerns.

I explained to him that even though I was doing well now, getting A's and B's, two years before I had flunked out with about a 1.2 GPA.

"I'll talk to them," he replied. "I'll make them understand that the Army made a man out of you and that now you are interested in education."

This he did, and I got into Cornell. Cornell was very well funded, so I was given a teaching assistantship, while my wife got a job teaching art. I started teaching my first course entitled "The American Experience," a freshman level class of nothing but ideas – my forte. The professor was Milton Konvitz whose claim to fame was that he had written the constitutions for many emerging African nations as they became independent in the 1960s. Konvitz was the quintessential absent-minded professor. He could never remember my name, and he was usually off somewhere in his own world. The system at Cornell University was to have a famous professor, published in his field, teach once a week in an auditorium setting. He would give a lecture to maybe 200 students, and then they would break that large group down into 20 or so participants led by teaching assistants twice a week for three credits.

I was pretty far out on drugs and alcohol at the time, and I thought that this course was basically a waste of time. So I said to my students, "I am not particularly interested in this course, but if you want to have philosophical discussions, let's meet at each other's house or dorm room. Whoever hosts can be responsible for a jug of wine and some ganja to smoke."

I went to another teaching assistant and said, "If any of my students are really interested in the course material, I will send them to you, and if anyone just wants to talk philosophically, you can send them to me."

As it turned out, we had some great, stoned, philosophical discussions. I told my students, "If you show up every week, I will give you an A. If you decide you do not want to participate, I will give you a B." That worked out well for my first year at Cornell.

My second year, I got a new boss and had to teach a more rigorous course, which meant I had to read the course material and attend his lectures to know what was going on. Tough life.

I still told my students, "As long as you come to my two classes per week I will give you an A. If not I'll give you a B." That worked out well, at least at first. My last semester, the professor got wind of what I was doing and called me into his office.

"Listen, Mahoney," he said. "If you give everyone an A, I will have to fire you. If I don't see some Cs and Ds, there will be consequences." So I gave some Cs to the people I did not like and who had not come to class.

I did not graduate in 1972, at the end of my two years at Cornell. I was supposed to complete one course in statistics, but the reality was that I was so stoned and burned out that I could not grasp the subject matter. So I took an incomplete for the course and dropped out. I told everyone that I wouldn't take a political science degree from such a conservative institution, which was why I was leaving only one course short of a master's degree. I eventually did complete the course work, though, and received my degree in 1975.

Meanwhile, my marriage was going to hell. The deal that I had made with Sue and myself – one day sober for school and my wife, the other for being crazy and drunk and doing what I wanted – had worked well for these last couple of years. But it was starting to wear thin on both Sue and me.

Around the time I graduated, I took a good hard look at the business world and decided it was definitely not for me. Right at about this time, a friend I had grown up with called from Aspen, Colorado and said, "Bill, you gotta see this place. This is the craziest town I've ever seen. It's like nonstop partying."

"I'm there," I said. That's when I knew that I was going to divorce Sue. I wanted more; more women, more freedom, more everything. My alcoholism was calling to me.

Don't get me wrong. Sue was a wonderful human being and a good Al-Anon. She had been more than willing to put up with me. We had spent the previous summer traveling around Europe, during which time I was getting more and more depressed. So I finally told her, using that old chestnut, "It's not you. It's me," which was true enough, I guess, although bottom line, I just wanted out. "We can still be friends," I added.

Although the separation devastated both of us, I felt I had no choice. We went through the divorce proceedings and it was finalized by the time I was through with my course work. Some would say that after almost 4 years of marriage, with Sue working and me going to school, I left her because I no longer needed her. But that would not be true. The real truth was that while I loved Sue, I loved alcohol more.

## Chapter 6: Heading for Colorado

After the call from my friend in Aspen, I bought a Volkswagen van and drove it out to Colorado. There was a girl who lived on our street in Dryden, New York who, when she found out I was driving out west said, "Great! Could you give me a lift?" She was a high school student who had just graduated. I agreed to take her with me.

Back then, anyone sharing a Volkswagen van had to have sex with the driver. So we spent the whole trip out there having sex. She may have been reluctant, but to me it was no big deal. Halfway to Colorado I pulled into a campground and parked next to a brand new black BMW motorcycle. There was a black tent set up next to it, in front of which sat a person in black leathers and a black helmet. I was fascinated, and when I went over to introduce myself, she took her helmet off and her hair fell down to her waist. I was in love.

She had, she told me, just come from Alaska along the Alcan Highway. She was on her way back to New Jersey. We spent the whole evening talking, during which I realized this woman wanted to get laid. "I don't fuck," I told her, putting into play that classic pick up line; "I make love." Which worked like a charm. I also invited her to turn around and follow me to Colorado. "Let's see what happens," I said.

And so she did, riding her brand-new BMW directly behind me. The teenage girl who had started the journey with me faded into the background. I honestly don't remember what happened to her.

In any event, me and "Motorcycle Liz" got to Colorado where we stayed in a teepee on a mountain overlooking the town of Carbondale. I reconnected with my friend Bob O'Shaughnessy, who was the youngest person ever to get his own seat on the American Stock Exchange. He'd been working on Wall Street since he was 16, and the day he turned 21 they gave him his own seat on the exchange. By the time he turned 25, he was totally burned out. He had made a ton of money, so he dropped out and bummed around the world for two years. Somehow, he ended up in Carbondale, where he bought a gas station with the last of his money. Why? I do not know, since he had no interest in cars. He also bought a piece of land upon which he had set up the teepee in which my new girlfriend and I were crashing.

It was an enjoyable place to stay, but with one caveat; it was hard to get off the mountain to get down to the bars. But we stayed there for maybe two months before "Motorcycle Liz" started getting bored. So she left and, finally on my own, I started my life in Colorado.

I moved into an apartment above a garage with a guy named Willie, who was hiding out because he was wanted for murder in New York. Willie was a nice guy, although I have to admit, he was kind of crazy.

I was living on the money I got from selling my house in Dryden, New York, money which I managed to squander pretty quickly. With my last two or three thousand, I bought a firewood business from a local guy who wanted out. The purchase included a 1951 2 ½-ton Chevy dump truck, a 1950 half-ton pickup, a 1960 quarter-ton pickup, and a few Stihl chainsaws.

It also included a large pile of firewood from an old apple orchard that the seller had cut and stored on a piece of land owned by a 90 plus-year-old Italian woman from one of the original Carbondale families. I asked her how much she would charge me to keep storing the wood on her property.

"If you let me steal a little bit of your apple wood, you can store it for free on my property," she offered. She would sneak out, steal one piece of apple wood every couple of days, and bring it back to her house to burn, so it was a good arrangement for both of us.

I placed an ad in the Aspen paper for the firewood, and I included the phone number of the Black Nugget Saloon in Carbondale, because that's where I was spending all of my time. Every once in awhile, the phone would ring and I'd get a "Hey, Mahoney, it's for you." So I'd answer and take down the person's information and deliver the order to them. It was a good business and it kept me busy. If it was a large load, I had this 2 ½ ton stake-bed truck that could hold 2 ½ cords of wood. I'd hire some of the drunks in the saloon, buy them a case of beer, and together we'd load and unload the truck. This worked out well for everybody.

My friend Bob O'Shaughnessy knew these retired Hells Angels from his California days. They were apparently wanted in California, so they showed up in Carbondale to hide out for a while. It was a good place to hide out, because the town had exactly one cop.

These Angels were the craziest people I ever met. But they were drinkers like me, so we started hanging out together in the Black Nugget Saloon and, of course, we got along great. Also, they had drugs to sell, including PCP, which was meant as a tranquilizer for elephants and rhinoceroses. They gave me some to sell, but when I took some, I realized how pure it was. Somebody could easily die from an overdose of this stuff. A tiny bit would just lay a person out.

I was getting drunk one day in the bar and I had the last of a little bit of this stuff in my pocket. Three guys whom I did not know came in one day and said, "I hear you have some PCP." Without thinking, I pulled the drug out of my pocket and said, "Here, just take it. I don't want to sell it. Be careful. It's very powerful."

I handed over the packet, and the three of them went into the bathroom. They laid out some lines like it was coke, and snorted it. They immediately fell over, right there in the bathroom, and could not move. Somebody called the police and an ambulance came and took them to the hospital. One of them said, "Yeah, Mahoney sold it to us," so the police started looking for me.

I had this friend called "Mushroom Michael" who, like me, had a firewood business and, also like me, dealt a little dope on the side. Michael was living up above Aspen on the backside of the mountain at 10,000 feet. He had built three Styrofoam domes and a number of people were living with him up there. He stored his firewood on the property.

We decided to exchange residences for a while. Even though the Carbondale cops and the Garfield County Sheriff were looking for me, Aspen was in a different county with a different police force. So, if I was living in Aspen, they wouldn't know and vice versa. This was before everything was computerized.

It worked out fine except that I was now living above 10,000 feet in the middle of winter. We had to park maybe a quarter-mile below these domes and then walk up there through the snow, which could sometimes be chest high or higher. This got to be very difficult, and finally I couldn't take it anymore. I complained about it to Mushroom Michael who said, "Listen, I have a contact in Washington State who runs a hothouse for the perfect get-high psilocybin mushroom offshoot."

I called a buddy I had gone to college with in New Paltz and told him about these mushrooms, and he said, "Great! Bring 'em on out. I can sell them."

Mushroom Michael fronted me ten pounds of mushrooms which had to be flash frozen and kept under dry ice for the drive back to New York. I had a '64 Plymouth Fury. I put two Styrofoam containers of mushrooms and dry ice in the trunk and began the drive back.

Somewhere around St. Louis, the front end started rattling very badly. I ignored it, kept on driving, and then the front right wheel fell off. I stopped, got out and opened the trunk to see what tools I had. Pretty soon, a cop car pulled up behind me. "What's going on?" he said. I showed him the wheel. Then he looked into the open trunk and asked, "What's in the Styrofoam containers?"

"Oh, nothing," I said, nonchalantly slamming the trunk shut.

Miraculously, he let the matter drop. "There's a machine parts shop off the highway up the road," he said as he got into his cruiser and drove away.

I looked at the wheel. The spindle was chewed up, so I took it to the machine shop and got new ball bearings, put the spindle back on, and drove back on down the road. Luck of the Irish. I made it back to New Paltz without further incident. I stayed with my friends in New Paltz and started selling mushrooms.

These mushrooms were incredibly powerful. You could slice off a little piece, eat it, and start hallucinating immediately. As for me, I was eating them by the handful and got pretty far out of it. In fact, I got so high that I forgot to get dry ice, and the mushrooms melted into a sloppy mess. Now they were not salable. So my friends and I had an omelet party where I just dumped the remaining mushrooms, probably a pound or two, into the eggs. There were a dozen of us there, and everybody ate some and we all got really trippy.

The problem for me now was that I did not have enough money to pay Mushroom Michael back. So when I returned to Aspen, I just laid myself at his mercy.

"Tell you what," said he, "Why don't you just give me your equipment for the firewood business?"

So I gave him all the equipment, which I don't think was worth as much as the mushrooms, but it was enough to satisfy him and we remained friends. However, now without the firewood business I was kind of at loose ends.

## Chapter 7: The Gift Shop Caper

I continued hanging out in the local bars, hustling pool, and playing Liar's Poker, which I was doing one night in a bar in Basalt, Colorado. One of the players was this older guy who used to come into the joint with a suitcase full of money and throw it around at the poker table. He didn't care if he lost. He would just laugh and keep on playing.

I was kind of intrigued by him. His name, if I recall correctly, was Bob Schetter. I befriended him and tried to warn him not to throw his money around. "Someone's gonna steal that suitcase," I told him.

One day in 1977 or '78, I got a call from him. His son, who knew how bad an alcoholic he was, had had him committed to a detox center in Newcastle. The place sort of reminded me of an old chicken coop. Bob needed someone to sign him out and be responsible for him. I was happy to do that for him.

He took me to his home, which was up on a hill overlooking Basalt, and proceeded to tell me his whole life story. He had been a gay man before it was okay to be gay. Before he came out, he told me, he had been married to a woman who was diagnosed with cancer. He watched as she wasted away to the point where he finally had to administer pills so she could die with some dignity. This, he said, had turned him off to women.

Bob had two gift shops in downtown Aspen. At "Aspen Unlimited Ltd." he sold little tourist things that said "Aspen" on them; tee shirts and stuff. He said, "How would you like to run my stores for me?"

He may have been a bad alcoholic, but he was a smart businessman. He had legally cut his son out of the business and he needed someone to run his stores for him. "I'll teach you the business," he said.

"Fine," I said. "Sounds good to me."

Turns out, he was a marketing genius. He had spent his entire working life opening stores, designing shelving, and determining where and how best to place merchandise for maximum effect. He showed me how to stock the store with the best-selling items placed at eye-level starting on the right. "If an item is moving slowly," he instructed, "move it down so the prime space is filled with the best-selling items." Lots of hints and tips like that.

Then he cut me loose running these two stores for him. They were money-making machines. At the time, Aspen was coming into its own as a very exclusive resort. The local joke was that the billionaires were pushing out the millionaires. The town had originally been a ski resort in winter, while the off-season was dead.

But now, tourists were there all year long, and Bob's stores were making money hand over fist. The deal I made with him was that we would cook the books and take 20% off the top of the gross receipts. The money was just flowing in. We would split it 60% for him and 40% for me.

Bob was such a drunk that he only had a few hours of coherence in the middle of the day. He was suffering from last-stage alcoholism, so he could not sleep more than three or four hours at a time. He would have to get up and drink in order to pass out again. He was in no shape to run the stores.

I was as bad an alcoholic as he was, but I was young and strong. As drunk as I was, I could still function reasonably well. This being Aspen in the 1970s, there were a lot of drugs around. I had plenty of money and so I started doing vast quantities of cocaine, in addition to the booze I was consuming. I was spending as much as I made.

Bob liked to go to Las Vegas to fly his freak flag in the Vegas gay community, and I would accompany him to keep him out of trouble. While we were there, I looked around and realized that there were lots of opportunities to make money. So I said, "Hey Bob, let's open a store in Las Vegas. We can sell stuff with 'Las Vegas' printed on it."

"Good idea," said Bob. So we opened a shop in the Las Vegas Mini Mall right across from Circus-Circus on the Strip. The store turned out to be very successful. I would fly there from Colorado every month to do the ordering, straighten up the shelves, and empty the bank account. Since the bars in Vegas never closed, neither did I.

Our store manager would find me after three or four days, passed out drunk somewhere, and he'd put me on a plane back to Colorado. This worked out well for about a year. As for Bob, when he'd go to Vegas, he just wanted to party and go to the gay baths and stuff. He was really in love with me and I knew it. But I was not gay and so could not give him what he needed, emotionally or sexually. He finally fell in love with someone he met in Vegas. The upshot was that he fired me so this guy he met could take over. I had been too drunk to see it coming.

## Chapter 8: Lori

Around this time – 1974-75 – I met a woman who lived above a head shop in Carbondale. This was pretty much before anybody in Carbondale except for the hippies knew what a head shop was. We ended up in bed in her apartment and I have to say, this was the only time in my life that I had to do the old routine of grabbing my boots and my cowboy hat and going out the window to stand on the ledge. That's because as we were lying there, we heard a voice from down below call, "Hey Lori!" It was her ex-husband, whom she told me was six-foot-four and huge. "Quick! Hide!" she whispered. So I grabbed my stuff and went out on the second floor ledge.

I'm thinking, "If he sees me, I'll have to jump and maybe break a leg or something."

He came upstairs. They yelled for a while. Then he left and I came in off the ledge. I said to her, "Y'know, I should get out of town and maybe you should too." She agreed, and so we went back to New

Paltz, my old college town, and moved into a cabin in the middle of an apple orchard.

While I was there, I went to the college and told them the story of how I had gone to Cornell but had dropped out before getting my degree. All I needed was a course in statistics to complete it. There was a professor there who taught a course in non-parametric statistics, which is statistics without the heavy mathematics. So I took his course and ended up getting a B in it. I sent a letter to Cornell and got my MILR Degree – Master of industrial and Labor Relations – dated 1975.

One night Lori and I went out to a bar where they were having an amateur strip night. Lori got up and stripped to the music and everybody cheered. She had never done it before. In fact, she was a very shy woman…beautiful, but shy. She loved it. As it happened, there was an agent in the crowd who came up afterwards and said, "Listen, if you want to do this for a living, here's my card." And so, she called him.

This guy had a route that went from New Paltz into the Catskills along Route 17 West through rustbelt towns like Rochester, Syracuse, and Endicott. They all had these redneck roadside bars with a five-dollar cover charge and beers for a buck fifty. They would put a stripper like Lori on a little stage and she would take off her clothes, dance to the music, and get tips and a salary. So she was making really good money, and I was driving her around from gig to gig.

I found out right away that I could not hang around these bars because everyone would want to fight me. "Oh, so you're the boyfriend, eh?" So we would come into town, check into a motel, and I would drive her to the bar where she was working that night and leave her off.

    Then I'd go get drunk at another bar, and pick her up at closing time. Once in awhile Lori would tell me, when I came to pick her up after the bars closed, that she had a customer who was willing to pay her for sex. She would vet this person closely and make sure he was not a threat. Usually it was just some horny local businessman. She would tell me what motel they were going to, and I would wait outside. It usually didn't take long. Lori had her tricks to make a man climax quickly, and she had the rare ability to separate sex from her emotions. After it was over, I would pick her up, she would describe the encounter to me, and we would both have a good laugh. This sometimes led to sex on our part. Usually though, we would have sex in the mornings, when I would pound away to lessen the effects of my hangovers.

    These road trips went on for about a year. She was always paid in cash, so we had plenty of money. After a trip, we would go home to the doublewide trailer we had bought in the Catskills, where we would hang out with friends...especially one guy named John who was something of a genius. Lori had always been attracted to brains, so she started sleeping with him behind my back. This was virtually the only time in my life that a woman ever cheated on me while we were going together. She finally told me about it, though I couldn't really blame her, since by then I was almost worthless as a sex partner. I was getting way too drunk and could not perform on a regular basis. I could see that John too was becoming an alcoholic, but I could not tell Lori that. As it happened, I was right about him. He died a couple of years later as a result of his drinking.

After months of this, she finally said, "Bill, you're the love of my life, but I can't put up with you getting drunk all the time." I gotta say, this really hurt, because Lori was also the love of *my* life. She loaned me $500, which in those days was enough to buy a car and drive it back to Colorado.

Many years later, after I had sobered up, I got in touch with her. She had moved to Denver with her husband, (the two of them had gone to chiropractic school together) and they were planning to open their own practice together in Englewood. I told her, "I have that $500 you loaned me, and I want to pay you back." They needed money, so she was glad to receive it. One of the tenets of Alcoholics Anonymous is that you try to make amends to the people you may have hurt because of your drinking. It felt good to pay her back.

## Chapter 9: Adrienne and the Joker's Inn

Back in Colorado, it wasn't long before I was broke again. I was just hanging out in the bars, hustling pool, and playing liar's poker – anything to keep up my habit. Around this time, I met a woman named Adrienne. She was older than I, but she had plenty of money, plus a beautiful house in the hills outside of Carbondale. So I moved in with her. Like me, Adrienne was a stone alcoholic.

She also had a real estate broker's license, so I decided to go to real estate school and get *my* realtor's license. The two of us would put a bottle of vodka and a container of orange juice into a cooler with some ice and drive around looking at real estate. We stayed too drunk to really make any money at it, so we decided to open a bar instead.

A guy we knew named "Uncle Dale" had a saloon in Glenwood Springs called – what else? – "Uncle Dale's." Business was good, but his son was stealing all the money and putting it up his nose. So the bar either went into foreclosure or else Uncle Dale just walked away from it. We bought it, re-christened it, "The Joker's Inn," and started making money hand-over fist. My friend Kevin O'Reilly used to joke that I was "on full scholarship," living in a big house, co-owning a bar, and drinking my fill of free booze.

On the other hand, I was getting better with my drinking, or at least *I* thought so. For years, I had drunk until I blacked out. But when I got the bar, I had to count the money and restock it at 2:00 AM, so I had to stay somewhat sober.

I *was* doing a lot of drugs, however, which I got from an unusual source. The local police and DEA started sending a progression of undercover narcs into the place, thinking maybe I was into dealing drugs. They were easy to spot. I told them, "I do not deal drugs. I only deal alcohol. But if you have any samples, I'll see if I can tell people I know about them." I would get grams of really good cocaine from them, snort it, and tell them that I could not find a dealer to buy it, but if they had some more, I would keep trying. So I was recycling a lot of confiscated drugs through my system thanks to the DEA.

This being the '70s, we had a dance floor and played disco music, which I hated, but every night we would be packed with kids dancing to the music. Then another place in town opened with live music, and we died. No business.

So I thought, "Well, why don't we turn the place into a country disco?" I went out and bought $200 worth of plowshares, horse collars, and other country stuff for the décor. I also bought $200 worth of country music albums which, being a kid from Brooklyn, I knew nothing about. We put an ad in the paper advertising ourselves as a country disco, and pretty soon, the place was packed again.

All the big ranches outside of Aspen, Rifle, Carbondale, and Glenwood Springs, were hiring Mexican cowboys. The Mexicans loved the joint, the music, and especially the mechanical bull, which we rented and had installed in the bar. They would bet on who could stay on it the longest. I might have been so drunk that I couldn't walk, but I *could* run that damned bull. I got to where I knew when to throw a rider off and when to keep the momentum going. We put a bunch of old mattresses around it so nobody got hurt when they landed. It was sweet and everybody had a good time. Except, of course, when the fights broke out.

The police were in there all the time breaking up the bar brawls, and at one point, they threatened to pull our liquor license. Adrienne got scared and we started arguing. A lot. One night I came home blacked out drunk and, well, I guess I hit her. I've never been an abuser, but I'm sure that's what happened. She ended up throwing all my clothes out on the lawn and calling the cops. I picked up my stuff and drove back into town. Living with Adrienne had lasted two years.

## Chapter 10: Mountain Rivers Detox

I was 34 years old. I had no money, having left the shoebox full of hundred dollar bills in her house when she threw me out. So all I had was whatever was in my pockets, some clothes, and my beat up old station wagon. I started calling friends.

The third phone call I made was to Bob O'Shaughnessy. He was staying at the Mountain Rivers Detox Center in Glenwood Springs, trying to sober up. (His pancreas had been failing for years due to his drinking.) I told him that Adrienne had called the cops and they were looking for me.

"Why don't you check in here?" he said. "It's anonymous. They won't tell the cops where you are."

In AA, they say that every successful recovering alcoholic has a kind of miracle moment of clarity about their condition. My miracle moment came as I was standing outside of the Lariat Saloon in Glenwood Springs, waiting for Bob O'Shaughnessy to pick me up and take me to detox. I looked into the window. The

Lariat was a place I had visited many times. It was the only bar in town open at 7:00 o'clock in the morning so that all the geriatric drunks could go to get a couple of shots to help them lose the shakes before going home. As I stood there, I realized that something was about to give, physically, emotionally, and spiritually.

"If I go in there and have a drink," I said to myself, "*that* will be me – a broken down human being, drinking in the morning to lose the shakes." My drinking had finally turned on me.

Bob picked me up and took me to Mountain Rivers. I was still pretty fuzzy at that point. All I knew was that this was a detox center, that I could leave at any time, and that while I was in there I couldn't drink. I signed myself in.

Somebody handed me a big book called *Alcoholics Anonymous*, and said, "Here. Read this." I could not read for three or four days because my mind was still so fuzzy. But when my head finally cleared, I read it from cover-to-cover and learned all about the 12-Steps. I decided to give it my best shot.

Nobody told me how hard the 12 Steps were to accomplish, or that this would be a lifetime commitment. In Alcoholics Anonymous they say "one day at a time." Stay sober one day at a time. I knew that I could never commit to staying sober for a lifetime, but staying clean for just one day at a time made sense to me. Every day I would say to myself, "No drink today. I can go for one more day." I did that day-after-day, and the days started adding up.

Mountain Rivers had just opened in Glenwood Springs, so there were not many people with a lot of time in sobriety. The management got us going out to

AA meetings right away. We were a tight-knit group and we would all pile into someone's car and go to the meetings together.

I was having a great time, hanging out with this bunch of people who were a) as crazy as I was, and b) newly sober. There were not many meetings in Glenwood Springs, so we would drive to Vail to hear Betty Ford speak. She had just opened the Betty Ford Clinic, and she was a great speaker. Or we would go to Aspen and see many famous people at the meetings. Aspen was 40 miles south. Vail was 60 miles east. Rifle was 30 miles west. We would go out every week for meetings, and I just had a great time. My sobriety date is May 10, 1981. Ever since that day, I've been sober and I'm just thrilled no longer to be drinking. I had had a great time during my years as a drunk, and now I was having a great time sober.

I am still in touch with some of the people from that time, including Kevin O'Reilly whom I see at AA meetings in South Florida. Kevin is a retired lawyer who I drank with for almost 10 years in Colorado. He sobered up about 10 months after I did because he was facing three DUI charges and was about to lose his law license.

I met Kevin when I first moved to the Aspen Valley. He was a public defender, but his heart was in helping people stay out of jail. I was a bar room drinker, as was Kevin. He often kept me company at the local bars. He was up for anything that had to do with having fun. We hung out together for almost 10 years in the Aspen Valley. It was Kevin who, on one occasion, kept me from having to go to jail.

One night back in 1977 or '78, I was drinking at the Black Nugget Saloon when I got a call on the payphone from Kevin saying he was in jail in Glenwood Springs and could I come and get him out. He had run his car into a ditch and the cops found him and took him to jail for driving drunk. He knew I would be at the Nugget Saloon hustling pool. So when I got the call, I jumped in my car and headed for the jail, which was about 12 miles away. I got there and bailed him out.

We decided that since I myself had a trial date set for the following morning, we'd better not get separated. So we drove to his house, which was in the middle of nowhere, and started drinking Scotch and talking strategy for *my* trial. I'd been charged with assault several months prior to this for hitting a guy with a beer bottle. The guy weighed 250 pounds and was a notorious fighter. I had pretty much cleaned him out on the pool table and I could see he was getting madder and madder and wanted to beat the crap out of me. I was sitting in a booth drinking a longneck Bud and as he reached over to grab me, I picked it up and smashed it into his face, thereby giving him about 84 stitches. He was such an animal that he was still able to pull me out of the booth and was on top of me dripping blood 'til his friend pulled him off and took him to the hospital. He reported the incident to the police and got a professional photographer to take pictures of the face I'd rearranged for him.

I was known by the police in Carbondale as a drunk and a troublemaker, so when they realized it was me, they decided they would try to put me in jail for a year. I hired my lawyer friend Kevin O'Reilly to defend me.

So anyway, when we finished the bottle of scotch, we realized it was 5 o'clock in the morning and we were drunk on our asses. All we had time to do was shower and shave and drive to the courtroom, which was about 20 to 25 miles away. Kevin had a bottle of schnapps...and so what does a good Irish alcoholic do but drink himself sober with the schnapps? Which was what we did.

We got to court, where I immediately passed out on the defendants table. Kevin was picking the jury and the next thing I knew he was yelling and pounding on the table and demanding a mistrial. The prosecutor had screwed up by telling the potential jurors that I had hit the plaintiff with a beer bottle without prior cause or provocation. The judge realized that in legal terms Kevin was right. He had no choice but to declare a mistrial. So by 10:30 that morning, we were in Doc Holiday's Saloon drinking Bloody Marys and laughing about the whole situation.

The prosecutor was so embarrassed that he decided to retry me. Within the month, I was back in court. We picked a jury and. because it was a small town, we both knew a couple people who were on it. This, of course, we did not disclose. Kevin used what came to be called the "Barroom Defense," which was later written up in the Colorado law books as established law. Basically it says that if you go to a "bucket of blood saloon" where you know that there are many fights and you pick a fight, you deserve what you get. On that basis, the jury found me not guilty...not exactly innocent, as Kevin was at pains to point out, but not exactly guilty either.

Kevin and I were drinking buddies for 10 years in Colorado, and now for the past 10 years in Florida we have been good friends in our sobriety. I mainly see him at AA meetings. I am breaking Kevin's anonymity here, but I do not think he would mind.

While we're on the subject of old Colorado drinking buddies, I should mention my pal Jerry Fletcher, who was already in Mountain Rivers when I got there. His problem was that he would go on a running drunk and then drive somewhere and get into a car wreck. He wrecked untold numbers of autos before he finally sobered up for the last time, probably in 1982. He ended up going to school to become an electrician. He was very successful at it in the Aspen area, where he would find wealthy clients and overcharge them mercilessly.

One of his victims was a man who had invented a way to move checks through the banking system more quickly. He had sold the business for $50 million and had bought himself a ranch outside of Aspen where he kept lions and tigers in cages. Jerry charged him over $50,000 for two weeks worth of work bringing electricity to a gazebo 100 yards behind his house.

Meanwhile, I was putting in a satellite dish for the guy for a few thousand dollars. I was jealous, but being in AA, I was trying my best to live honestly, so it was okay.

Before I move on in my story, I should probably mention another good buddy whom I met in Florida; Jim Medlicott. When I bought my first Florida property back in 2010, he had just been thrown out of his house by his long-term girlfriend, and he needed a place to stay. I had an extra bedroom, so I invited him to move into my condo.

He's a hard-working guy who drives tanker trucks for a living. I met him through AA and we quickly became good friends. He's a cigar smoker who always has a chomped-up cigar in his mouth. It was Jim who got me hooked on cigars, although he has since given them up. I, on the other hand, am now totally addicted to them.

    I give him a lot of credit because he's serious about his sobriety and he has a good work ethic. He comes from a well to-do family. They own a printing business. Jim was drinking and drugging away when his mother died. She left him enough money so he would never have to work again, but did not leave him any part of the business. He is now enjoying life on a yacht, playing golf, and going to AA meetings.

# My Life in Pictures

**My Folks, Leona and Frank Mahoney**

**Me and My Big Brother Jerry**

**First Communion**

That's me...Row 2, second from the left

Christmas with my brother Jerry

**Pre-hippie High School Pic**

**New Paltz**

**Cornell**

**Vietnam**

## My First Marriage

Lori

**Adrienne**

**Vietnam travel buddy Ron Eich and girlfriend, Gail**

**Baha'i Friends from Around the World**

# A Shot at Redemption

This article appeared in the Denver Post on November 8, 1993

**The Plane**

**Always a fan of vintage automobiles**

Second Wife Ladjamaya and her son, Akin

In Siberia with the Ultra-Marathon Runners, (That's *Bam-Bam* the truck in the background)

That's me on the left. My Siberian business partner, Sasha, is on the right. Second from right is Victor, General Secretary of the Baikal Amur Mainline Railroad

Our Ski-Helicopter in Siberia

Landing Strip at Lukla, Nepal at the base of Mt. Everest.

Guggenheim Museum, Bilbao, Spain 2003

## Florida Buddies

Kevin O'Reilley

Jim Medlicott

**On Vacation with Joan in Barcelona**

**The Jets**

## Chapter 11: Deer Haven

About a year after I got sober, my mother died. I went to my parents' house in Boynton Beach, Florida to meet up with my dad and brother for the funeral. Jerry told me that my mother had been complaining about how bad my father's memory was becoming. Now, seeing him face-to-face, we realized how serious the situation had become.

He had blocked out all memory of his life, from being married, to having children, to being a fireman – basically his whole life since childhood. My brother, who was in the middle of a very successful business career and had two young children, said he would take my father home with him to New Jersey, try to keep him well, and look for a good place to put him.

My dad had always been a controlled drinker. Three or four drinks and he'd say, "Okay, I've had enough. I'd better not drink anymore." He was Catholic, and according to Catholic theology, getting tipsy was okay, but getting drunk was a mortal sin.

Except for a few occasions at parties, he would never get drunk. But being Irish, alcohol was part of life, and so he would get tipsy on a regular basis. But now, he had lost the ability to control his drinking and to know when enough was enough.

By the time my brother took him in, he was drinking over a pint of scotch a day. Then he would wander off looking for a liquor store, and Jerry would have to go and find him. Jerry is a workaholic and this was distracting him from his work. He travelled a lot for his job, and he also had two small children, so it was not a good situation for them either.

He called me in Colorado and asked if I would take Dad for a few weeks while he looked for a memory care center for him. He flew him out to Colorado, and I took him in. Dad was still coherent when he arrived, although he did not know where he was or why. Life had been hard on him in recent years as he tried to take care of my ailing mother while his own mind was failing. The stress had finally snapped his brain. He did not remember being married or having children, but I think he was happy just being single. I saw his moving in with me as an opportunity to make amends for what I had put him through as a kid.

He had a decent retirement income from being a New York City fireman. He was also drawing Social Security, while I was working hard, putting in and servicing satellite dishes. So money was not a problem.

Dad had blocked out all memory of the fact that he had had children, so he thought of me as just a good friend. As it turned out, we got along just fine. I was renting a four-bedroom house in a little town near Glenwood Springs called No Name. I had two roommates, one of whom moved out when I brought my father in.  Dad was still coherent enough to be able to be by himself while I was away installing satellite dishes in Aspen.

We lived close to Interstate 70, which was still being built through Glenwood Canyon at the time, and sometimes Dad would wander down to the highway looking for where he had grown up on West $28^{th}$ St. and $10^{th}$ Ave. in Manhattan.  I'd get home and go in search of him.  After this happened a couple of times, I had a conversation with the flag women in which I explained that Dad had Alzheimer's.  They agreed to hold him on the side of the road until I could come to pick him up in my newly restored 1948 Buick Roadmaster.  I would put him in the back seat like I was the chauffeur driving him around.  He loved this as long as the weather was good.

At some point, Dad decided that he wanted a woman in his life, which I knew was virtually impossible.  I thought fast and said, "I'll get you a dog."  I found him a little poodle mix and we called him Blackie.  Dad and Blackie quickly became inseparable.  He would get up in the morning, have cereal for breakfast, and put a bowl of cereal down for Blackie.  Blackie would lap it up.  Dad would forget that he had already fed him and put down another bowl of cereal and so on.  So Blackie began putting on weight.  I would get up later and wonder why he wasn't hungry and why he was getting so fat, until I realized what was going on.  The two of them were inseparable right up until dad died.

This arrangement worked fine for about 2 ½ years.  By then we knew that dad had Alzheimer's and that at some point he would become incontinent and forget how to use the toilet.  At that point, I would have to put him in a memory care center.  I also knew that once they go into memory care, patients become worse because they cannot deal with a new environment.

I looked into Colorado law to see what the rules were for opening a full service non-medical elder care facility. Not all that complicated, I discovered. So I leased the whole property we were living at in No Name, which consisted of four cabins and the four-bedroom house I was already sharing with dad – and gave it the name "Deer Haven." I did the paperwork to make it legal, put an ad in the paper, and started getting calls. I very quickly moved nine elderly patients in, and hired a woman to live there and cook and clean and take care of them.

I found out that it was possible to get a grant to help with this. So I applied and, with the money, bought a 15-passenger van to take everybody around. The first woman I hired lasted about six months, after which I found a couple – Gertie and Bob – to take over. I was very lucky to find them. They were a loving couple and, as an added bonus, Gertie was an excellent cook. She would either bring the meals out to the cabins, or serve a central meal in the kitchen in the big house. This arrangement lasted over two years, during which time my father got progressively worse. The whole idea was to make sure that dad would have the best care possible until he died.

Alzheimer's is a very strange disease. Fibrous tangles keep growing and growing into deeper and deeper parts of the brain, until finally even the immune system stops working. People who live 'til the very end finally die from pneumonia because their immune system is out of whack. That's what happened to my dad. He finally got pneumonia and went into the hospital. By that time, he had no vocabulary, and really no cognition of who or where he was.

His doctor wanted to know if he should take him off of life support. "Is there any chance, if he lives through this, that he will have any quality of life at all?" I asked.

"None whatsoever," replied the doc.

"Well, I guess you might as well pull the plug," I said. Dad was dead within the next 24 hours. My brother flew out for the funeral. I gave Deer Haven Inc. to Gertie and Bob who had done such a loving job of taking care of dad in his final years.

After dad died, I learned that Jerry had been taking care of his money for him. I was pleasantly surprised when he told me that dad had accumulated about $280,000, which Jerry and I split. Around this same time, my aunt died and left me about $60,000, which meant that I now had around $200,000 to work with.

## Chapter 12: The Real Estate Biz

I decided to go into the real estate business. I had been doing fine putting in satellite dishes and filling and servicing fire extinguishers, but I knew that real estate had more potential to make money. I do not believe in the notion that hard work makes people rich. Rather, it's a matter of good luck and timing.

In 1981, a strip-mining operation had opened up in Parachute, Colorado to make oil shale for Navy jet planes. The mining company lost its contract with the Navy and shut down the operation. Many people had moved into the surrounding area because of the oil shale boom, and when it shut down it devastated the economy of Western Colorado. By the time my dad died in 1988, Rifle National Bank had gone into receivership and HUD (Housing and Urban Development) had begun auctioning off foreclosed properties…just when I came into my inheritance. (Like I say, "Good Luck and Timing.") I ended up buying a 20-unit apartment building in Rifle, plus a beautiful property on Rifle Creek that consisted of two large houses, four log cabins, and two trailer homes. The apartment building went for $100,000, with 20% down. The Rifle Creek property cost me eighty grand, also with 20% down. I was off and running in the real estate business.

    I kept those properties for three or four years, by which time the Western Slope economy had rebounded and real estate prices had jumped sky high. The apartment building was low-end, my tenants mainly Mexican laborers. The Rifle Creek property was beautiful, and so it always stayed full. By 1991, I had come to the conclusion that prices for properties on the Western Slope were peaking, while Denver's real estate market had crashed and property there was now very cheap. So I sold both properties in Rifle, the apartment building for $420,000 and the Rifle Creek property for $180,000. I now had enough capital to go and play in the Denver market.

    Denver has always been a boom and bust town. It relied on oil, and in the late '80s there was an oil bust, which meant that real estate in Denver could be had for incredibly cheap. I found a realtor and told him that I wanted to get the most bricks for the buck. He started showing me properties in Five Points, Denver's historic black neighborhood.

    As we walked down the alleys, we would see junkies shooting up, while they would see these two white boys and smile and say, "Hi. How you doing?" I remember thinking, "Boy, this really is a cow town." I grew up in Brooklyn where if you ran across a junkie shooting up in an alley, he would shoot your ass. So I thought, "If this is the worst Denver has, I can deal with it."

    We found two properties to buy. One was in Curtis Park. It was called Curtis Park Flats and it consisted of nine railroad apartments made up of just three rooms in a row, one behind the other. The building was boarded up. At $40,000, the price was right, and I bought it for cash on the barrelhead.

The other property I bought in Five Points was a 15-unit apartment building that was going for $60,000. It, too, was all boarded up. I had done my homework and knew that Denver's city government wanted boarded up properties in Five Points rehabbed...which meant I could acquire very low-interest city money to get the job done. So I applied for it.

I had no idea what I was doing, but I filled out the paperwork and, sure enough, I got 50% rehab money for the Curtis Park building (or a hundred percent if I finished it to their satisfaction). I also got a hundred percent rehab money for the 15-unit building. The mayor at the time was Wellington Webb, who was black. He wanted to put money into the city's black neighborhoods.

At about the same time I began rehabbing those buildings, I found out that there were a total of 75 units under foreclosure and coming up for auction. So I found out where the auction was and went, figuring I could get all 75 for about $200,000. That's how cheap real estate was in Denver at the time. I thought, "For that price, if I knock the buildings down and sell the bricks on the corner I could make my money back."

So I went to the auction where, unfortunately, there were two other parties bidding against me; one guy and his partner in person at the auction block in the courthouse, the other over the phone. Between those two, the price kept going up. I got caught up in auction fever and ended up paying $280,000 for the property. I got screwed.

When it was all over, I realized that I was $80,000 short of what I needed. The bank had agreed to loan me 180 grand. I had $20,000 I could put down, and so I needed $80,000.

The next day, I got a call from my mentor in this writing endeavor and soon to be good friend, Don Morreale. He had been one of the guys bidding against me at the auction. We sat in my car and talked turkey. "Listen," he said, "there are 15 units in the package that are being rented by Cambodian refugees." As it happened, Don had spent many years as a young man travelling and studying meditation in that part of the world and, like the Cambodians, he was a Buddhist. He said, "I understand these people and what they need." (I certainly did not). "Most of them don't speak English. The toilets are on the fritz, and the places are falling down and full of cockroaches."

To be honest, I did not know what to do with this property. But I did know what to do with the empty, boarded-up buildings; just get city money and find a contractor to fix them up. I said, "Do you have any money?"

"As a matter of fact, he said, "I just sold a building and I have $80,000 cash..." which just happened to be the exact amount I needed to close on the entire package of 75 units I had bid on at auction. So we made a deal and we have been best friends ever since. I love it when a plan comes together like that.

## Chapter 13: The Welcome-Home-Vietnam-Veterans Parade

Although I was investing in Denver, I was still living in Glenwood Springs. In 1986 a friend of mine by the name of Ron Eich called me from New York and said, "Bill, there's a Welcome Home Vietnam Veterans Parade coming up in Chicago. I think we should go."

I had not dealt with my Vietnam experience in the nearly 20 years I'd been back, so I agreed to meet him there. Something like 200,000 Vietnam veterans showed up. I was astounded. These were the guys who had fought the war – people my age, a lot of them strung out on drugs or burned out from PTSD.

Many, myself included, had not really dealt with the trauma we'd endured there. There was a half-size Vietnam War Memorial at the Chicago gathering. We saw people going up to it and, finding the name of a comrade who had died, would just collapse in tears while other vets made a circle around them to protect them as they wept.

The parade came the following day. I couldn't help but compare it to how it had been when we had returned from the war back in the '60s and were spit on and called baby killers.

This time around, however, it became a ticker-tape parade and the people working in the high-rise office buildings on State Street came out to congratulate us and to welcome us home and thank us for our service. The tears started flowing and everybody, including me, put on shades to hide them. It was, needless to say, a very emotional time. It took a long time to go from "baby-killer" to "thank-you-for-your-service," but today I wear my Vietnam veterans cap and I get all kinds of people coming up to thank me and congratulate me.

It was a good weekend and a healing experience for all of us. Right after the parade, Ron and I went into a bar to get a drink…in my case, a Coke. While we were sitting there, this guy came up and said, "Can I sit with you?" The place was packed, so of course we said yes. He said, "I have never told anyone this, but when I was in Vietnam, I got shot in the gut and spent a long time in the hospital recuperating. When they let me out, I put on my Class-A uniform and went back to my home in the Midwest. When I got off the bus there was a protest going on, and when they saw me, these protesters, they spat at me and said 'Baby killer,' and one of them even kicked me in the stomach. It opened up my wound. I had to run. I could not defend myself. I was still recuperating from the gut wound. I never told my parents what had happened. I just went into the bathroom, stanched the blood and never told anyone about it."

That was a lot of people's experience coming home from the war. You can imagine what that did to the guy, emotionally and spiritually. By the time he finished his story, we were all crying.

## Chapter 14: A Baha'i Epiphany

I had a rental car and, after the parade, I dropped some people off at the airport. After that I still had four or five hours to kill before *my* flight. I knew that Sheridan Boulevard, which went north from Chicago along the lake, had some beautiful homes on it. I've always loved architecture, so I drove north to see these homes. At one point, as I was rounding a curve in the road, I came upon this oasis of serenity, a beautiful white domed building with gardens all around it. I pulled into the parking lot and walked up the steps. At the top stood a black man with the sun behind him and a beautiful blue aura all around him.

Now, I am not big on auras. I usually don't see them, but because my emotions were so raw and wide-open from the parade, I saw his. He said, "Welcome to the Baha'i House of Worship. All faiths are welcome here. You're welcome to go in and pray." So I went in and it was incredibly peaceful in there. I sat for a while, and when I came out the man said, "Do you have any questions?"

I don't remember the details, but every question I asked and he answered made sense to me. Basically what he told me was, "This is one world and one God. If you believe in one God then this really means that there is only one religion. All the major religions are a continuation of the same spiritual message that God leaves for man on a regular basis."

This made perfect sense to me. "Well, okay," I said, "so now what should I do?"

He took me downstairs to the library and gave me a couple books. "Read these," he said. "Fill out this card and someone will contact you."

I went home to Glenwood Springs and started telling everyone I knew about how Christ had returned, just as he said he would in the Bible, in the form of Baha'u'llah, the latest profit of God. He had died in 1892. I did not know any other Baha'is in town, and I was starting to lose my enthusiasm. It's tough to be a member of a religion when you're the only one.

But then I got a call from a Baha'i named Tom Hunn who lived in Grand Junction, about 90 miles away. "I got a card that you filled out in Chicago," he said. "Do you want to become a Baha'i?"

"I *am* a Baha'i," I said.

"Well then, why don't I come to your house and we'll talk." Tom was a jeweler, and a wonderful man. He came to my house in Glenwood Springs and we talked, and it turned out he was *also* an alcoholic – a sober alcoholic like me. He had written to the Universal House of Justice, the governing body of the Baha'i faith in Haifa, Israel – to ask if it was okay to be an alcoholic and a Baha'i. He said that he believed that the Alcoholics Anonymous book, written by Bill Wilson, had been divinely inspired. The House of Justice wrote back and said, "Absolutely. This is a wonderful program, and please stay active in Alcoholics Anonymous."

So with that, he was satisfied that the Baha'i faith was true. And now, talking to him, so was I. We met together several times after that to study the writings of Baha'u'llah. In the next few years, I met many other Baha'is in the area, and once there were nine adult Baha'is, we formed a local spiritual assembly, which is the administrative arm of the faith.

Abdul Baha, the son of Baha'u'llah, had visited Glenwood Springs on a trip through the Americas in 1912, so every year we would commemorate his visit. For the 1990 commemoration, a woman named Ladjamaya Green did a one-woman show called, "The Black Experience; A Cry for World Peace." She was very dynamic, and I was attracted to her. That weekend, we fell in love.

She was living in Maine at the time, so we wrote and phoned one another for the next few months until she could come back to Colorado for a visit. We spent a weekend together and decided to get married. On January 1991, we were joined in holy matrimony at the Hotel Colorado, an historic venue on the Colorado River where Abdul Baha had stayed on his trip through America in 1912. The marriage would last for 13 years.

## Chapter 15: The Russia Adventure

     By this time, I was doing well in real estate and going back and forth to Russia. I had first gone there in 1987 with a group called "Creating a Sober World." Our mission was to bring the AA message to the Russians. This was before the breakup of the Soviet Union, and Russia had, and still has, a terrible problem with alcoholism. There was no AA in Russia back then. We would meet in the large hospitals where they housed alcoholics. They had no idea what to do with them. They would just detox them and put them back out on the street.

     Alcoholics Anonymous offers a spiritual message, one which the Soviet alcoholics were very receptive to…as were the doctors who treated them. We were very successful. We started AA meetings in Moscow, St. Petersburg, and Kiev in the Ukraine. I have lost touch with many of my Russian alcoholic friends, but I believe the groups we started are still growing and very active.

The translator for our delegation was a guy named Sasha Frolov. He said, "If you can bring people to Russia, I can book hotels and airline tickets for them." At the time, it was not possible to get into Russia except through *InTourist*, the government tourist agency. Sasha was the head of a Komsomol group, which was a young communist club.

Sasha worked for the Director General of the BAM Railroad and Baikal Amur Mainline Railroad, which was, at the time, the largest construction project in the world. Their mission was to build a train line north of the Trans-Siberian Railroad, because the Russians were afraid that the existing line was too close to China. They were concerned that if there was a war, the existing line could get overrun. Also, they thought of it as a way, indeed the only way, to open up Siberia. So they built the Bam Railroad over the permafrost, 3000 kilometers from Omsk to Vladivostok.

Sasha's father, who was a long distance runner in his 50s, wanted to put together a trans-Siberian ultra-marathon, and he asked me to help him. We could, he said, use the road that ran alongside the tracks for the run, and make history by being the first Westerners ever to cross Siberia on foot. He also promised us the use of a private railroad car.

So when I got back to the States, I put an ad in *Ultra Marathon Runners Magazine* and people started calling me, saying they would love to go on this adventure. Working with Sasha, we got the proper visas. Twelve of us flew to Moscow – nine American runners and an Australian who was one of the top five ultramarathon runners in the world, plus a chiropractor for sports medicine, and myself to serve as coordinator.

Once there, all of our expenses were covered by our Russian hosts.

We flew from Moscow to Ulan Ude at the southern end of Lake Baikal. Lake Baikal, incidentally, contains 20% of the world's fresh water. It's an incredibly beautiful area, very primitive. From there we flew to Novo Sibirsk, which is located at the northern end of Lake Baikal. We were given the use of a private railroad car on the Bam Railroad, and an enormous Russian truck we nicknamed "Bam-Bam," with six-wheel drive to travel the rough roads.

The original plan was to run east all the way to Pyongyang, North Korea. But in the end, we could not get the proper visas, so we were not able to enter. We ran east along the railroad, covering 50 to 100 miles per day.

The Soviets had built the railroad by going to their southernmost provinces – Uzbekistan, Tajikistan, Kirgizstan etc. – to recruit construction workers. As an inducement, they told them they would build Soviet cities every 50 to 100 miles along the route where they would be provided with housing, schools, and an automobile. This was a huge inducement because at that time there was a minimum five-year wait for a car in the Soviet Union. They moved whole tribes of Uzbeks into the new towns.

In every city we ran through, we got a huge welcome. We were the first Westerners to go through this area. As the organizer, I was invited by the local chief to a banquet. With Sasha serving as translator, the chief offered me a business opportunity. "Listen," he said, "I control all of this area. Moscow has nothing to do with it. If you can find someone to buy the products we make here locally, we can split the profits."

After that, every town we went to, Sasha would write up an agreement and I would sign it. In one town, the chief took us to the top of a hill and said, "See this *taiga* (forest)? It goes on for 100 miles. I control this entire forest of pine trees. If you can sell them in the West, I can ship them via the railroad to Vladivostok, on the Pacific Ocean."

Another chief controlled a mountain full of *charito*, a purple semiprecious stone. If I could get the right paperwork to get it out of the Soviet Union, he told me, I could sell it and we would split the proceeds.

Yet another town had control of tons and tons of lingonberries. As things played out, I ended up controlling probably half of the products that were local to Siberia

The Soviets who managed the forests were selling to the Japanese, whom they hated because they would only trade cheap radios and televisions for their products. They knew the Americans would pay cash, so they were happy to deal with me. I came back from that trip and started the "Soviet-American Cooperation Society." I opened an office with a secretary to try and sell these products.

In launching this business, I discovered a good life lesson: there are very few early adopters out there. All the lumber companies I contacted, their first question was, "What is the percentage of moisture in the trees? Can they be milled?" I said I didn't know, but that the Russians were willing to sell hundreds of square miles of pine trees for very little money. Nobody jumped on it.

Same thing with the lingonberries. I called Kroger and other food chains popular in the Midwest where the Scandinavians (big consumers of lingonberries) had settled, and they asked, "Well is it FDA approved?"

I said, "No, you would be the first to get these out of Russia." Again, no one was interested,

Another thing I tried to sell was helicopter skiing. I spent four days in an ME8 helicopter, a Russian troop carrier that could hold up to 16 people, and looked for places to helicopter-ski around Lake Baikal. The mountains in the area were spectacular and no one had ever skied there.

We landed on mountains that looked promising and had some locals ski down them. Then we flew down to pick them up. We mapped the area and were ready to take Westerners skiing at a very cheap price. But when I put an ad in *Skiing Magazine*, all these so-called daredevil skiers would ask if we had insurance, and how were the local hospitals?

"No one's ever skied these mountains before," I explained. "You would be the first." I thought this would be enticement enough to get people to go. But *no*! Everyone said, "Well after you've done this a few times, call me back. I would love to do it." No one wanted to be first.

I could not get anything going with all these incredible opportunities in front of me, so I was getting frustrated. On the other hand, by this time, the Soviet Union had collapsed, and the country was open to – among other things – religions coming in to proselytize, which was a perfect opportunity to spread the Baha'i faith. I contacted Baha'i headquarters in Haifa, Israel, and they asked me to come over and consult with them. They informed me of what was going on in Russia, and how other religions were rushing in to proselytize. They asked if I would be willing to lead some Baha'i trips into Russia and, of course, I said yes.

I put the word out that I could get visas, hotel rooms and plane and train tickets if anyone wanted to go. Over the next three or four years, I arranged for over 500 Baha'is to enter Russia. Sasha booked all the train, plane, and hotel reservations to move people around. I went to Russia 17 times during that period. It was a very exciting time for me.

I was flying in and out of Denver, which was a long trip from Glenwood Springs to the airport, so Ladjamaya and I decided to build a 5000 square foot house in Genesee, just west of Denver at about 7400 feet altitude.

My real estate business was doing very well. By that time, I had rehabbed over 60 units and they were all rented and throwing off a lot of cash flow. I hired a woman named Eddie May Wolfolk to be my property manager. She had started a company called Faith Management, and she was very well known and respected in Denver's black community where my apartment buildings were located. She kept them rented for me. I felt like I was doing some good by providing safe and affordable housing for the black community.

I would come back to Denver for two or three weeks at a time to organize another Baha'i trip to Russia, the Ukraine, and the Central Asian Republics of Uzbekistan, Tajikistan, etc. In Russia, we would go to the parks during the days to hand out Baha'i pamphlets. People would read them and be interested right away because their system had failed them, and they knew it. We would explain to them that although Communism had been a noble experiment, it had lacked a spiritual dimension, and was thus destined to fail. Altruism without some form of spiritual underpinning is not possible. This made sense to them.

We would invite them back to the hotel that night for tea and cookies and explain the Baha'i faith to them in more depth; in a nutshell, "Humanity is one, and it is time for you to join the rest of the world."

Everywhere we went we would spend a few days to a week and leave behind a Baha'i community, with a place to meet, a treasury, and a local spiritual assembly of nine people. In this, we were relying on the nearby German Baha'i Community to go in, consolidate, and teach. Unfortunately, they were not ready to do this, so it became problematic. Even so, many communities that we started in that part of the world are still functioning and growing.

In 1994, we went to Arkhangelsk in northern Russia where even in the summer it was cold. We'd hand out pamphlets on the streets and people would look at them and say with a shrug, "Oh, another religion," and throw them in the gutter. We realized that the time for the Russian soul to open up to new ideas was over, and that Western notions of consumerism had taken the place of idealism.

On the Arkhangelsk mission, I shared a hotel room with a German Baha'i, actually a Persian guy who had lived in Germany for over 30 years. His Baha'i community, he said after a long day of handing out pamphlets, was the same size as it had been when he first got to Germany.

"After the Berlin Wall came down, we went there to hand out pamphlets," he told me. "The people coming from the East would stop and read them and ask questions. We would have meetings every night in the hotel, and we were able to create a Baha'i community on a week's trip." He was an engineer, and after the trip to Berlin he had gone back home to work. "Six weeks later, I went back to Berlin to hand out more pamphlets," he said. "At the Brandenburg gate, people were still streaming through, going from East to West. But this time, they would take the pamphlets and say, 'Oh. Another religion,' and throw them down in the street with contempt. Or they would ask us for directions to the nearest television store." My friend realized that it took only six weeks for the Communist experiment to go by the wayside, and for Western consumerism to fill the people's souls.

At that point, I stopped going to Russia and returned to Denver to concentrate on my real estate business, which was doing very well even though I wasn't there much of the time. I'm not big on the notion of God's hand on my shoulder, but I really felt – and still feel – that I was doing the right thing by spreading the faith, helping to get Baha'i into Russia.

## Chapter 16: End of a Marriage and Rise of Desert Rose

After each trip to Russia, I would return home and be surprised that things were going so well. I mean, you sign a million dollar plus contract to rehab a building and then leave, fully expecting everything to have gone to hell by the time you get back. Invariably, though, the projects were going fairly smoothly in my absence. So I felt like this was because I was doing the right thing in life.

When I came back in 1994, a building just northeast of downtown Denver became available. It had just over 20,000 square feet and had been boarded up for 10 years. It was nicknamed "The Pigeon Building" because the windows had all been broken out and hundreds of pigeons were nesting in there. Pigeon feathers and pigeon poop was everywhere. There were also a lot of feral cats living in the building and feeding on the pigeons. The upper floor was not finished, and overall the building didn't show very well for a prospective buyer. My kind of project.

I put in a bid for $100,000, which was accepted immediately. I thought, "This is incredible. How cheap can real estate get in Denver?" The building was on the corner of 25$^{th}$ and Champa, just five blocks north of downtown. So I rehabbed it into 23 apartment units and it came out very well.

I had great cash flow with all the units I owned at the time – about 75 to 80 "doors" as we called them. I was netting between $15,000 and$18,000 a month. By the time I turned 65, I had Social Security, Medicare, and money in the bank, but I was getting burned out on dealing with managers and tenants. And now my marriage was falling apart.

I loved Ladjamaya very much, but I longed for deeper emotional companionship. She was wonderful at getting and maintaining acquaintances, but would back off if you tried to get too close to her. After 12 years, it became too painful for me, and I finally decided we needed a divorce. Ladj agreed to it.

I wasn't worried that she would try to hurt me financially, but I also knew that I needed to be fair with her. So I gave her a substantial cash settlement, plus a doublewide trailer to live in at the Desert Rose Baha'i Institute near Casa Grande, Arizona, 60 miles south of Phoenix on the road to Tucson.

I had been on the board of Desert Rose for many years, and one of our ideas had been to retire there. So I found a top-of-the-line doublewide trailer abandoned in the woods and made an offer of $6000 for it. It was a low-ball offer but, surprisingly, the seller accepted it. One of the reasons it was so cheap was that nobody believed it could be moved. It was located in the hill country about 30 miles from Eloy. To bring it in, the seller had built a dirt road that had subsequently been washed out by the rains.

Nonetheless, I was able to find a moving company that was willing to give it a shot. "Yeah we can move it," said the movers. "It will probably scrape the bottom but we can get it out for ya."

"Go for it," I said. The move cost me five grand, but it was worth every penny.

I had it set up on a piece of land that I had developed next to Desert Rose and had sold to other Baha'is who wanted to live in the area. I had conceived of a plan to buy the land and drill three wells to supply the residents with water. There was a class of wells that could handle up to 15 houses apiece, as long as you didn't use them to irrigate.

During World War II, the flat Central Arizona Valley between Phoenix and Tucson had been used to grow food for the war effort. The land sits on a huge aquifer just 400 to 600 feet below the ground, so they dug these huge irrigation wells every half mile all over the valley.

After the war, however, the engineers realized that the plate over the aquifer had collapsed up to 16 feet because they had been draining it so quickly. They decided to ban large wells. From that time forward, only wells that could handle up to 15 houses were allowed to be drilled, and only one per square mile.

I owned 56 acres. I had it surveyed and carved up into parcels upon which I was able to drill three wells. I put in a road and had it paved, and then sold it to Baha'is for exactly what I paid for it. Plots went for between $10,000 and $25,000, depending on size. In addition, anyone who bought had a spiritual obligation to pay Desert Rose an additional $10,000. In this way, we were able to raise over $400,000 for the community.

Since I was already in Arizona developing for the Baha'is, I figured I might as well buy a burned-out building in downtown Phoenix and develop it into 18 lofts. This was an old 1928 hotel, which was very historic for Phoenix, though it had gone downhill and become a flophouse. To make matters worse, somebody had started a fire in it that had turned it into a burned out shell.

But the brick structure was sound enough to rehab. I put together a team of architects, a real estate marketer, and a construction team to rebuild it. It was very successful and won an award for the best project to uplift downtown Phoenix, which at that time was just coming out of a huge slump.

I ended up buying another building and making seven lofts out of it. This was during a bull market in Phoenix, so when I sold the properties, everyone who bought one was able to flip it and make a lot of money. At the end of the first of the two projects, the contractor wanted to get the last 10% – about $170,000 – that I owed. They gave me an invoice that was way more than I owed them. I decided I would fight it, but at first tried to negotiate a deal.

Instead, they ended up suing me, so I kept the hundred-and-seventy grand. Now they wanted over $200,000. So I got on my high horse and decided to fight it. I hired a lawyer. The lawsuit went on for eight years. I had no insurance for a lawsuit after the project was finished, and the contractor, who should have had insurance, was let out of the lawsuit. So there was no one left with deep pockets.

Their lawyers ended up going to the Arizona Supreme Court eight years later. It came back that the contractor should be kept in the lawsuit, so it became active again and went into arbitration. The arbiter was a guy who had been fired by my indemnifying insurance company (who would not indemnify me anyway) for being drunk on the job, which I found out after the fact.

I hired a lawyer who was, at that time, in the middle of a murder trial. Big mistake…because as it turned out, she knew almost nothing about real estate law. I lost in the arbitration. Big time. The arbiter put every penalty, interest, and fee on me that he could. I ended up owing $400,000. I had that much money and rather than fight it, I just paid the damned thing. So all those years in Phoenix, I never made a dime.

Despite all the crap, it was a very successful project in that it was creative and even got written up in Arizona Architect Magazine. It also won the Dreamer Award as the project that had had the most impact on downtown Phoenix. It was located on the west side of downtown, which had not yet been developed. After that, the Phoenix city fathers knew that the West Side would be the next big development area.

## Chapter 17: Taking Wing

Some years before all this happened, and after I had started to make some decent money in real estate, I decided I wanted to learn how to fly. It would be an expensive hobby, but I was just turning 40 and had always envied pilots. Learning to fly was kind of a scary proposition, but I kept thinking, "There are 10,000 planes in the air at any given time," which harkened back to the principle lesson I had learned as a soldier – "If they can do it, you can too."

So I took lessons and started flying around the Colorado Rockies, from Glenwood Springs to Aspen, to Crested Butte, to Paonia, and a lot of other little towns along the way. It was truly exhilarating. I got my license around the time I started developing in Phoenix.

There was also a practical reason I wanted to learn to fly. It was a long trip to drive to the Denver Airport from Glenwood, and then to fly from there to Phoenix where I would rent a car and go take care of business. But after I got my pilots license, I could just jump in my plane – a *Cessna 182* – at the Glenwood

Springs airport, which was just a few minutes from our house, and fly to Phoenix Sky Harbor Airport in three to 3 ½ hours. I kept a car at the airport so I could just hop in and go.

Everything was going swell until one day when I was trying to get out of Phoenix. It was around 110° out there and I was in line to depart behind nine 737s. They all had air conditioning. I did not. I had two bottles of water with me. That was it. The line took maybe 45 minutes, during which time I went through both bottles. I really thought I was going to pass out from the heat.

When I finally took off and got up into the air, the engine was so overheated that the fuel system began vapor locking and the engine started missing. I headed north, and before long the motor was missing pretty badly and I was getting scared. I thought to myself, "If the engine quits, I'm a dead man."

Down below, in the mountains in Northern Arizona, I saw a little airport and decided to land. The mechanic there told me that a vapor lock was no big deal. "Give it a couple hours to cool down," he said, "and you'll be good to go." I was not particularly reassured.

"Easy for you to say," I told him. "Why don't you come up and fly with me before I leave the area?" So he did and the plane was fine and I flew back to Colorado without further incident.

But that was the end of me flying into sky Harbor Airport, Phoenix. From then on, I would fly into Eloy Airport near to where the Baha'i Institute was located. I kept the car at Desert Rose and put a doublewide trailer on the land to use as a home base.

From there it was only an hour's drive north to Phoenix, which was convenient enough.

During the time I was getting my wings, I was building the 5000 square-foot home in Genesee, in the foothills west of Denver, where Ladjamaya and I had moved after we left Glenwood Springs. After the move, I began flying out of the airport north of Denver, which is now known as Rocky Mountain National Airport. It was only about 20 minutes drive from the house in Genesee, so it was still convenient to fly from there to Phoenix. As an added bonus, since I was using the plane for business it was a great tax write off for me.

During this time, Ladjamaya's son, Akin, was getting married to a woman whose family lived in Ames, Iowa. We decided to go visit them during Christmas that year. Halfway there, we ran into a weather front and had to land and spend the night in a motel in a small town in Kansas. The next day the weather was still bad. I had never gotten my instrument rating because it was not a good idea to fly a single engine on instruments in the mountains. My plane was a turbocharged *Cessna 210*. It was a good plane for basic transportation purposes. It flew at about 200 miles an hour.

It was the day before Christmas and the weather was still pretty bad, so I put Ladjamaya and Akin on a bus to Ames so they would be there in time for Christmas, even if I could not be there with them.

Christmas morning the weather was stable, but with a low deck of clouds. I decided to "scud run," which is pilot-speak for running under the clouds. The air was calm, so I thought I could make it. As I flew towards Ames, the clouds kept getting lower and lower, which meant I was flying illegally at five or six-hundred feet above the surface. When I saw the airport runway at Ames, I thought, "Boy, am I lucky."

I was lined up with the runway and I thought, "Just let me get the damned thing down." The *Cessna 210* has a retractable gear, which means you have to put the wheels down to land it. There is a control system that beeps at you at two or three hundred feet above the runway. Well I was so nervous that when I heard it beeping, I just thought, "Whatever that is, just let me get the plane down and I'll worry about it after I'm on the ground."

In the aviation community there's a saying that goes, "There are pilots that *have* landed, and pilots that *will* land with the gear up." So I guess this was my turn. I made a perfect one-point landing on the belly of the plane and skidded down the middle of the runway. It was Christmas day and fortunately there were no other planes around, so I was safe.

I got out, left the plane sitting there, and found a phone to call my hosts and tell them where I was. While I waited for them to come pick me up, I called the local police, who in turn called a tow company that came and picked the plane up off the runway and toted it off.

I went to the home of my future in-laws and had a good Christmas dinner, and naturally everyone was relieved that I was okay. A few days later, we got a commercial flight back to Colorado. I had over $30,000 in damage to the plane, but the insurance company did not total it because the wings were still intact. I had made a perfect one-point landing, so had just scraped the belly of the plane, bent the prop, and seized the engine because the prop was still running when I hit the runway. But like I say, the body was okay. It took a few months to get everything fixed.

I had a partner in the plane named Clem Koph. He was a good friend and understood what had happened. He said, "It's kinda like when a horse throws you off. You have to get right back on." So I rented a plane locally a few times to keep flying in order not to seize up mentally.

Meanwhile, Clem had decided that he had had enough flying for a lifetime and wanted out of the partnership. So I bought him out and got the plane to myself. I was doing well enough financially that it was no problem, plus it was a relief to have free access to it any time I wanted it.

I continued to fly it for a number of years until I moved to Florida part-time in 2010. It was just too long a flight from Colorado to Florida – 2400 miles – so I decided to sell the plane. By that time, I had been a pilot for about 25 years and had about 1500 hours of flying time under my belt, so I no longer had a passion for flight.

Later on though, I changed my mind. I decided that I still wanted to keep up my flying skills, so I started renting a plane whenever friends came to Florida for a visit. I'd take them up to show them the shore. Really, though, it was boring flying. I was used to flying in the West with its mountains and beautiful clear skies. By comparison, Florida was flat and dull.

On the other hand, it was kind of fun to fly along the Southeast Coast to see all the development that was taking place. I flew out of the Lake Worth Airport, which is just south of Palm Beach. It's now off-limits every time our illustrious president, Donald J. Trump, flies in to Mar-a-Lago in Palm Beach.

Since my friends only came to visit every few months, my flying skills started getting rusty. On a number of occasions, I would go to rent a plane and be told that I would have to take a lesson with an instructor before they would let me have it. At one point, I wanted to take my present wife, Joan, up for a flight, and got an instructor who was probably less than 25 years old. He thought he was a hotshot and had an attitude.

By then, I had been flying for 25 years, and so I took his instruction with a grain of salt, to say the least. At the end of an hour's instruction he said, "I'm sorry, but I cannot sign you off. Your skills are just too rusty."

"Well how much time will I need?" I asked.

"At least four hours and then we'll talk," he replied.

I had flown for years in mountainous territory, through all kinds of adventures, so I copped an attitude and told him off. That was the last time I flew. To be honest, I realized that my skills *were* getting more and more rusty since I was only flying once every few months. And so to my chagrin, Joan never got to fly with me. (But more on my present marriage later.)

## Chapter 18: Kickin' Back in Florida

As I approached my 65$^{th}$ birthday, I started thinking that maybe this would be a good time to retire. (After all, I was now officially a Medicare baby.) As a good Coloradan and Westerner, I was thinking that I might retire to Desert Rose Baha'i Institute or somewhere else in Arizona. But then it occurred to me that temperatures of 110 degrees are no laughing matter and could maybe even hurt you if you're not careful. That kind of dry heat is no fun anyway.

In 1972 my parents – good New Yorkers – had retired to Boynton Beach, Florida. I remembered visiting them in the 1970s and loving it. Plus my good friend from my drinking days in Colorado, Kevin O'Reilly, had retired to Boynton Beach and had a condo on the Intercoastal Waterway. I came down to visit him and fell in love with the area all over again.

This was in 2008 right after the economic crash of 2007. Real estate prices were half of what they had been the year before. I found a condo that had been for sale for $370,000. The seller had refinanced the place for $500,000 and then had taken the money and run.

This was fairly typical in Florida at that time. Colorado had not yet seen that kind of craziness in the real estate market, so when I realized I could buy the property for $200,000, I jumped on it. I had just sold a fifteen-unit apartment building in Colorado and had the money to pay cash. As an added bonus, the property needed very little work.

So now I had a Florida address on the Southeast Coast in Hypoluxo, which is just north of Boynton Beach. As I transitioned into retired life, I decided to sell off all of my properties in Colorado, which amounted to around 75 rental units. I found a realtor who had just moved to Denver from California. To him and his clients, real estate in Denver looked downright cheap.

I told him what I wanted to get for the 23 units that I owned at 25$^{th}$ and Ogden, and he listed it for 1.9 million dollars. I had owned these units for almost 20 years and had rehabbed them with very cheap city money that was now almost paid off. I ended up selling them for $1.7 million.

The buyer said, "What else have you got?" I told him about the 23 unit building I owned at 25$^{th}$ and Champa, and said I would take $2 million for it. His buyer bought it for $1.9 million. The first property was my jewel, and I had planned to – three or four years hence – turn it into condos, which would have been worth a cool 4 million bucks. But by that time I was pretty burned out, retirement was staring me in the face, and Florida beckoned.

I sold another building for $700,000, which left me with only one property, an 1896 Denver Square that I was living in. I finally decided to sell that one when an opportunity arose to buy a great house in a gated community in Delray Beach, Palm Beach County on the Southeast coast of Florida.

## Chapter 19: Falling in Love with Joan

During this time, I was going on eHarmony.com, the dating website, in search of a girlfriend. The second woman I met on the site was a medical doctor named Joan. I didn't really think that dating a doctor would work for me. My prejudice was that doctors were boring people who were only into science. Okay, they did a lot for humanity, but as a romantic partner, a doctor was so different from me that it would never work. But I bit the bullet and met Joan for lunch in an upscale restaurant in Denver's Cherry Creek.

She came in a little late and full of apologies. "Sorry I'm late," she said. "I was with my sister shopping at the Goodwill store. I love Goodwill."

Well for me that was a good omen for a relationship, and we hit it off right away. She was smart, funny, and beautiful. I felt myself drawn to her more than I initially thought I would. I was just looking for a date, but this one was what some of my friends refer to as "a keeper." We began dating and I was pleased to discover that she felt the same way about me.

Even so, we decided that we would not talk about the future or make any plans for at least a year. A year-and-a-half before we met, she had lost her husband of 26 years to emphysema. Being a caretaker and a doctor, she had retired to take care of him full-time. They had bought a house in San Carlos, Mexico to bring him down to sea level, because he could no longer live at Colorado's high-altitude. They spent six years or so in Mexico, during which he got sicker and sicker.

At some point they came back to Colorado to see a specialist and they were staying at her mother's house in the town of Golden. It was obvious, though, that he was at the end of his life. He could hardly breathe and he was in a lot of pain and could no longer walk. He died shortly thereafter.

When we met, she was still grieving, so I really felt I helped her deal with the loss and get over her grief. After a year of dating, she moved into the house I was living in. I began pushing her to get married, though she was still not yet ready.

Because I loved her, and because of my Baha'i faith which does not condone companionate marriage, I really wanted to tie the knot. Plus, as an old friend of mine used to say, "Always marry up," which I would definitely be doing if I married Joan. She was such a beautiful and wonderful woman that I kept pushing until she finally agreed.

We set a date that was almost a year off. We at first decided to get married in the Catholic Church, (Joan was a practicing Catholic). But, to get married in the Catholic Church, I would have to get an annulment from my first wife, Sue, whom I had married back in 1968.

"Fine with me," I said. I tracked down Sue, my first wife, who has since embraced her Jewish heritage. I was pleased to discover that she had three children and had lived a good life. "No problem," she said, "I'll do what it takes to get you an annulment."

When we finally got the paperwork from the Catholic Church, we realized what a medieval process the whole thing was. Sue was expected to reconstruct her whole life from our marriage 45 years before, and to sign a statement explaining why she wasn't still a Catholic, when she had never been one to begin with. She had only married in the church because I had insisted upon it.

"This is ridiculous,' Joan said. "You should not put her through this."

We started looking for a venue to get married in. Every place we looked at wanted so much money that we kept on searching until we finally discovered that the Denver Metro Baha'i Center would only charge us $400 to use their facility. The Baha'is had bought it from the Christian Scientists many years before. This particular Christian Science church was dying when the Baha'is bought the building from them. They were down to less than 30 members, none of whom was under 70 years old. The Baha'is got it for a song.

Upstairs there was a beautiful sanctuary. Because the Christian Scientists did not believe in crosses and religious symbols in general, it was more like a civic building than a church. Perfect for the Baha'is. So we decided to get married there.

Joan wanted a traditional wedding, which was okay with me. I asked my brother to be the best man and got my friend Don Morreale, who is a Buddhist teacher, to perform the ceremony for us.

With Don's help, we created a marriage ceremony. In the Baha'i faith, the marriage ceremony is only a simple sentence, with each person saying before two witnesses, "We will always abide by the will of God." Beyond that, the service can consist of whatever you want. We created a half-hour ceremony around that one sentence.

We said our vows before almost 100 guests from my Baha'i community, from my AA community, and from "The Jets," a group of guys who have hung out together for over a decade, and who every Friday morning feed the homeless a pancake breakfast at a facility called "Christ's Body Ministries."

After a wonderful wedding, we went to Cancun, Mexico, and then settled into married life. We spend our summers in Colorado and winters in Florida, travelling back and forth between the two. It's a beautiful lifestyle that suits us well.

We bought a house on a half-acre lot in Lakewood, just west of Denver, and love spending our summers there. Joan can do her gardening and I can lay up and do nothing, which is my preferred mode of living. Life is good.

## Chapter 20: Real Estate is Still in My Blood

Overall, life in Florida has been good to us. I have been there every winter for the past 10 years, and I'm happy to say that Joan likes it too. Although I have officially retired from the real estate business, I have continued to buy small houses in Florida. During my working years, whenever I did a project, I would put every penny I had into it. If it went belly up, I could end up broke. I did not want to go through that again, but real estate was still in my blood, and I couldn't resist buying some Florida properties that were incredible deals.

In addition to the condo I was living in when I first started going there, I bought two small houses, one for $80,000, and another for $143,000, and spent some money fixing them up. I've used them to generate income for the past eight or ten years, so it has worked out well. I also bought a house in the gated community on a golf course where Joan and I now live during the winter.

Back when I first started spending my winters in Florida, I took a three-week trip and met a couple who lived in Delray Beach. We became friends and as it turned out, he was on the board of directors for the

Hamlet Country Club. He told me that, though it was not final, it looked like they would be bought out by Seagate, an international tourism company that owned high-end properties in South Florida, including a hotel and a beach club. They did not, however, own a golf course. Hamlet Country Club was an exclusive golf community that was going bankrupt.

This was because just before the real estate bust in 2007 they had, with only 200 plus members, spent nine-and-a-half million dollars renovating their clubhouse and golf course. When the bust hit, there was no way they could keep up the payments. They increased the dues for mandatory membership to almost $2000 per month…at which point, the prices of houses went down dramatically.

I found a house on the property recommended to me by my travelling companions, Ed and Mary Lou Whalen. I got it for an astounding $77,000, spent another $75,000 to rehab it, and ultimately sold it for $520,000. I was the last person to pay the mandatory $40,000 fee to join the golf club, but even so, I still had less than $200,000 in this beautiful Florida property.

The house next door had been renovated by a Romanian doctor and her husband, who owned a string of strip clubs in Romania. They had decided to buy a much larger house elsewhere. We made them an offer on the house, which they accepted. This was the first time in my life that I paid close to retail for a house that did not need any work. But Joan loved the place, so we decided to do it. I rented out the house we'd been living in, which worked out well. So we are enjoying our new house and the Florida sunshine.

## Chapter 21: The Freedom Boating Club

After I gave up flying, it occurred to me that maybe I should get into boating. But as I checked it out, I realized that what people were telling me was true. Namely that owning a boat was like having a hole you poured money into...*lots* of money. I, however, found a cheap way to indulge my new hobby.

I discovered the Freedom Boating Club on Riviera Beach just north of Palm Beach. The club was relatively cheap to belong to; $7000 to join and $200 a month for use of up to a 45-foot-long boat, provided I did not use it on the weekends and was willing to pay for the fuel. Since I was now officially retired and had time to spend during the week, this arrangement made sense to me. In fact, I thought it was a heck of a deal. So I joined. They had 50 boats on hand, and they usually had the boat I wanted. I would invite friends to accompany me, which made it a lot more fun.

I would take the boat around the Palm Beach area along the Inter-coastal Waterway. The Marina was right across from Peanut Island, where President Kennedy, in his Palm Beach days, had maintained a secure bunker in case of attack. It is now a tourist site with tours of his bunker. Near Peanut Island is the Palm Beach Inlet, which takes you out to the Atlantic Ocean. I would either stay close to home if the weather was rough, or go out onto the Atlantic when the seas were calm.

There were a number of restaurants on the Inter-coastal where you could pull up, dock the boat, and eat lunch. I enjoyed doing that and so did my guests. Unfortunately, since these were rental boats, there were times when all of the electronics – including the depth finder – did not work properly. Since the Inter-coastal Waterway had shifting sands, it was hard to know for sure without a depth finder if the boat could go there. On three occasions, I hit a sandbar and bent the prop…, which meant that I would have to pay for a new prop to the tune of hundreds of dollars.

Each time this happened, I would complain to the owner of Freedom Boat Club. "Tough luck," he would say. "It's still up to you to keep the boat safe." After having been a member for three or four years, I bent the prop for the fourth time and got a bill for over $7000. I did some research and found out that this particular prop had already been rebuilt three times and, by law, you were forbidden to rebuild it a fourth time. "I'll pay for the prop but it's not my fault," I complained. "It's already been rebuilt three times."

So the guy got right up in my face and said, "This is the fourth prop you've bent and I'm sick of it. I'm not going to rent you another boat." So I called Visa to cancel the monthly $200 fee, and they called the owner with me on the phone. He admitted that he would no longer rent me a boat, but that I was still obligated to pay the $200 fee. As it turned out, Visa agreed with me. They even went back, collected six months of the previous fees, and refunded the money to me. That was pretty much the end of my boating career. I missed it for a while, but hey, life goes on.

## Chapter 22: Travels

    I always loved to travel and see the world, even in my drinking days. Interestingly enough, I drank less when I traveled because I wanted to remember what I saw. My first wife, Sue, was a teacher, so she had the summers off. I was a student, which meant that I too had my summers off. So we bought an Opal station wagon, hitched a pop-up camper onto the back of it, and traveled around the country, camping out as we went. We visited upwards of 46 states that summer, covering something like 15,000 miles in 11 weeks, and loving every minute of it.

    **Cajun Country:** The only state I would not go to was Texas. For some reason, I had a basic prejudice against Texas so I never traveled there until sometime in the '70s. I was dating a Cajun woman at the time, and we decided to go to Mardi Gras, which meant we would have to drive through Texas. As it turned out, the people were really nice and friendly down there. "Come on down y'all…"

Naturally, we got really drunk at Mardi Gras and ran out of money. So I called a friend in Colorado who was fairly stable and he sent me gas money for the trip back. As soon as we got it, we got drunk and spent the whole wad.

I knew my girlfriend Pam had family somewhere around New Orleans, so she said, "I really don't want to do this, but I can go and see my grandma and get some money. But I can't tell her I'm with a boy."

So we drove south into the *bayou* country, and on the way there, she told me that her's was one of the few Cajun families who owned their own plantation. It had been in the family for some 200 years. "We bred the local slaves whose descendents are now workers on the plantation. I grew up with this, so please be circumspect when you're talking to my family."

She let me off at a crossroads – not even a town – with a bar on each corner. "Go wait for me in the bar," she said. "I'll be right back to pick you up."

I think she just assumed I would go into the *white* bar. Not knowing which was which, and being a rebel anyway, I went into the *black* bar and asked for a drink. The bartender slopped two or three ounces of bourbon into a water glass and I thought, "I'm in the right place. This is great."

Then I started playing pool, and I honestly could not understand what the people were saying to me. It was such a southern black accent that I could not grasp one word of it. I was getting more and more frustrated and drunker by the minute, until finally a guy came up to me and said in language that I *could* understand, "Listen, what are you doing here? We've never seen a white guy in this bar."

He owned the local ambulance company, and had been in the Army, so I could understand him. In fact, we got along great. We spent the afternoon shooting pool and trading yucks.

Three hours after she'd dropped me off, Pam came back, went into the white bar, and saw that I wasn't there. Somebody told her that he'd seen a white guy go into the colored bar, so she came across the street, stood in the doorway, and yelled for me. When I came out, she was so upset she was shaking.

"I told you not to go near the colored bar," she screamed. I was so drunk by this time that I just laughed, not realizing that I was in way over my northern little white boy head. She would not calm down, and that was really the end of the relationship. We drove back to Colorado in silence on the money she'd gotten from her grandma.

Still, it was a memorable journey.

**Vietnam:** I still had more to deal with concerning my Vietnam experience and I wanted to go back to see the country 40 years later. I ran into my old friend, Ron Eich, who had also been there, and I talked him into going there with me. We set up a trip where we traveled to five or six cities, stayed in nice hotels, and had a great time. We even rented an elephant and took it for a ride.

We managed to locate one of the few memorials to the war in Vietnam, known locally as "The American War." This memorial featured a burnt-out Huey helicopter, a tank, and some artillery. Most people in Vietnam knew nothing about the war because the population now consisted mainly of younger people who had not even been born when the war was taking place.

I asked somebody about it and was told that when people got to our age, they retired them and put them into their backyards to tend their gardens and smoke ganja...which sounded good to me.

We went to Cu Chi, a battle site where American soldiers got slaughtered in such numbers that they stopped going in there to patrol. The people of Cu Chi were tiny, even smaller than the Vietnamese. They had dug tunnels all over the area going back even before the time when the French were there...hundreds of kilometers of tunnels. They would pop up out of these tiny holes that were so overgrown with grass you couldn't see them and mow down first the French, and then the Americans.

The women in these tunnels would take the expended brass and iron shells and file them down into spikes and iron crosses. Then they'd dig a hole, put them in, and cover them with vegetation. When our soldiers were on patrol and walking through the area, they would fall into these traps and the spikes would go through their legs and create terrible wounds. The Cu Chi people understood that for a patrol to lose a soldier who was terribly wounded and screaming took more manpower than if they just killed them outright. In the end, we stopped going on patrol in the area, and instead just flew over it and bombed the hell out of it.

Now it was a tourist area, one of the few in Vietnam and, for a few dollars, we could go down into the tunnels with a guide. They were not made for big Americans. I had to bend over to get through them. I covered maybe 200 yards before I had to get out, it was so horribly claustrophobic.

These people had lived for generations in these cleverly designed tunnels. In their kitchens, they had dug hundred-yard-long shafts to carry the smoke from their stoves up to the surface. As a result, we would fly over, see smoke and bomb it, completely missing their living areas.

During the Tet New Year's holiday of 1968, a cease-fire was declared. We thought, "Well we can relax." Meanwhile, the enemy were putting supplies – ordinance and whatever else they needed – into waterproof pouches and swimming them across the river. While they were doing so, we were busy getting stoned and spacing out. And we wonder why we lost the war!

On our trip to Vietnam, over 40 years later, we realized what wonderful people these were. We also realized how Communism had changed. The government still tries to control people's private lives, but they allow them the freedom to start businesses and prosper, which has made a big difference in the country.

I had blocked out my entire Vietnam wartime experience, including where I had been stationed. I remembered that it was somewhere outside of Pleiku in a point camp for Huey pilots and mechanics, but I could not remember where it was or what it was named. When I started asking the locals, they said, "Oh, that must be Camp Benjamin."

I asked a local guide to take me there. "We are not allowed to go there. It's off-limits, but it should not be a problem. Just bring some small bills with you to pay off the local Communist official."

And so we did. There was nothing left of the place. Everything had been torn down and was overgrown with vegetation, but I'm pretty sure I was in the right place. While we were there, a local official came driving up on a motorbike and the guide went over to talk to him. He passed him some money, which apparently satisfied him. He drove off without hassling us.

Another thing we wanted to see was the area in the Central Highlands where the indigenous Montagnard people lived. We discovered that the Vietnamese government had taken steps to insure that they kept their native culture, subsidizing them so that they could continue to live in their communal longhouses. Compare that to what we did to our own indigenous people whose culture we systematically wrecked. The Montagnards had not supported either side during the war. They wanted nothing to do with it. But they were a fierce people and we American soldiers were told to stay away from them.

We went to a Montagnard village and visited a local graveyard where the people were buried above ground in little huts with an altar to venerate their ancestors. As soon as I saw that, the hair stood up on the back of my neck, and I knew without remembering the particulars that I had been there on patrol during the war. I came to the end of the cemetery where there was a vista of a big valley of overgrown jungle. I had been in a firefight in this valley. It was a very strange experience.

Even so, the overall effect of this trip did not have much to do with redemption or putting the war to bed or anything. It was more just a good vacation. On the other hand, now as I'm thinking back on it, maybe it did have a little to do with redemption. I felt better having seen how well the Vietnamese people had recovered over 40 years later. They were doing very well economically and seemed happy, so there was at least some closure for me in seeing that.

**Chaco Canyon:** Another trip that stands out in my mind was one I took to Chaco Canyon in the 1970s to visit the cliff dwellings of the Anasazi people. I went there in my Volkswagen bus.

The Anasazi people lived in dwellings carved from the cliffs for protection against marauding bands. They lived there for about 400 years, and then disappeared sometime during the 1300s. We still do not know why they left, but it may have been because of drought.

Another story has to do with the American scout, Kit Carson, who went into the canyon because he knew that the Indians loved the fruit that grew there. Orchards had been planted by the Spanish some 200 years or more before this time. Carson set fire to the trees and waited at the top of the canyon. When the Indians realized what he had done, they came out in war mode and were slaughtered.

**India:** Another travel highlight was the trip I took to India, which I had always wanted to see. I was still single when I got the chance to go on an escorted trip with Overseas Adventure Travel with a group of a dozen or so people. We visited the highlights of Northern India including the Taj Mahal, Bangalore, and a tiger preserve. We got to ride rickshaws in Delhi and have dinner with the head of all the wildlife reserves in Northern India.

**Nepal:** A trip to Nepal was another fascinating adventure. I have owned a timeshare for years and have used it to travel to exotic places. So in Nepal, I stayed in a compound with a golf course just outside of Kathmandu.

While there, I met with the local Baha'is and was taken by motorbike around Kathmandu for two days to visit the stupas and temples.

I also took a plane ride up to the base camp at Mount Everest, a village called Lukla, which is the last place you can fly into if you want to climb to the summit. Otherwise, it would be a two-week trek on foot. It was a beautiful and amazing place. The runway is incredibly short and ends at the edge of a cliff. The mountains all around the camp are higher than 20,000 feet. There is no plane that can land on this runway except a Twin Otter, with reverse propellers that can stop on a dime. I was the only passenger on the flight I took.

Most days the airport is in the clouds, so only VFR (Visual Flight Rules) traffic is allowed. This means they cannot fly when the runway is socked in. So this was a rare treat. There were Sherpas there to meet the plane. I negotiated with one of them, telling him I was not a trekker, but that I wanted to see as much as I could.

"I'll take you to my village," he replied. "It is a 2 ½ hour walk up and down, but mostly up." We agreed on a price (I think it was $10) and we went with him to his village. His wife cooked us a lunch of lentils and a little chicken meat.

The village was very primitive, and consisted of maybe 50 to 100 houses. To build them, everything, including doors and windows had to be carried in. There was no electricity or plumbing. I observed that some of the houses were fancier than others. When I asked my Sherpa, he explained that those houses were reserved for those who had made it to the top of Everest – the elite Sherpas. He himself had never been to the summit. He would only take trekkers to the base camp at 18,000 feet. From there, the elite Sherpas would take them the rest of the way. He was a nice guy and he spoke some English.

  I stayed in Lukla in a very primitive hotel for two nights. On the third morning I was there, I got lucky again; it was clear, so we could fly out. As we took off, I looked down at the end of the runway and saw two or three wrecked planes. There was no way to clear the wreckage, so they had just been left there.

  Back in Kathmandu, I decided to fly west to the base camp of K2, another towering peak. We landed in a beautiful town that surrounded a crystal-clear blue lake. I spent two days there. The weather was not clearing up enough for us to fly out. I had to get back to Kathmandu to catch my plane back to the States, so I negotiated with a local driver to take me. It would be an all day drive.

  The driver said, "I want extra money because we'll be going through a dangerous area." The Shining Path Guerrillas were very active during this time, trying to overthrow the Hindu king of Nepal. They succeeded some time later when a member of the royal family killed the king and nine others. The drive was beautiful and peaceful, although we did see groups of armed guerrillas along the way. They didn't bother us and I had a great story to tell.

  **Singapore:** Another year, I used the timeshare to go to Singapore by myself. The city is as clean as people say it is. You can get arrested for spitting or throwing trash in the streets.

Singapore was truly amazing. A local politician in the 1970s had decided to take it from a Third World country to a First World country and he did a really good job of it. He created basic housing for the locals, a business haven for the corporations, and a lovely destination for the tourists. It has a huge port that is very active. The juxtaposition of the new high-rise office buildings and hotels, and the older housing for the locals, was striking to my Western sensibilities.

**Bali:** Another trip I took was to the island of Bali which is a round island about a hundred miles across. The reason it is such a popular tourist destination is that the Islamic Indonesian government has left the Hindu culture of Bali alone, mainly because it's a cash cow for them. The ancient Hindu traditions are fascinating, and they make up a large piece of Balinese life.

I hired a driver for $30 a day (which included gas) and he took me all over the island and explained the culture to me. He grew up a Hindu but did not actively practice it. He wanted to make money for his family. In the Hindu culture, he explained, everyone had to take at least one month off to worship, and to help the Hindu priests to build stuff. They required many sacrifices on the part of the people. Every house had to have its own altar, in addition to the altars in the large temples.

It was an interesting culture, and the island is pristine. I got to travel to the king's palace, which is a very modest affair. The gate was open when we drove by, and the driver said, "Let's go in." So we did.

We walked around and saw some concubines and people working the grounds. There was an open-air court where people with grievances could go and present their cases directly to the king, who would then decide the outcome.

**Chile:** Another interesting journey took me to Chile. I flew into Santiago with a Baha'i friend who had spent eight years living down there as a Baha'i Pioneer. He had many friends from his time in Chile, so we rented a four-wheel-drive, four-passenger Toyota and went down to the Lake District. The local people there belonged to the only indigenous tribe that had never been conquered by the Spanish. When the Spanish first arrived during the 16$^{th}$ century, they had slaughtered the people.

A small boy who witnessed the debacle realized that the only weakness the Conquistadors had was between their helmets and their breastplates. If you could reach them with a knife, you could slit their throats. The little boy grew up to be king, and he trained his warriors in how to defeat the Spanish. Seventy years later, when the Spanish came back south across the Brio Brio River and into this indigenous tribe's land, the natives were ready for them. They killed many Spanish and pushed them out.

The Spanish realized they could not conquer these people, so they signed a peace treaty with them and left them the land south of the Brio-Brio River. They have occupied it to this day, and remain the only indigenous tribe in the Americas never to have been conquered.

We were there during *Ridvan*, which is the Baha'i time when the local spiritual assembly is selected. We were brought to a hut in a small village to help with the selection. They were one person short and an old woman who lived there said, "I have a neighbor about a quarter mile away. Would you go get her?"

We found this old woman digging in her garden and we said to her, "We're electing a Baha'i local spiritual assembly, and we're one person short."

"Oh, I forgot," she said.

We walked back to the hut. I asked her how old she was and she replied, "I'm a hundred and three." But her neighbor said, "She's older than that," and then proceeded to tell us how 90 years before, they had been young women together selling vegetables in the town square. When they tallied it up (there were no official records), they figured she had to be older than a hundred and three.

The Baha'is had also established indigenous schools in the area, which they named after famous Baha'is. The children were getting a great education and loved being Baha'i. There were about 15,000 Baha'is in that area.

Tom Funk, the friend that I had gone to Chile with, was a rock star from the 1950s. He got so excited during our visit that he grabbed a guitar and started singing and dancing to songs from the '50s, much to the delight of the kids. The reason Tom had had to leave Chile was that he got involved in a gold deal where he lost all his money. So he had to go back to the States to earn a living for his wife and three small children

**Israel:** Another place that I loved going to was Israel, which is the administrative center of the Baha'i faith. Its headquarters is in Haifa. Back when I had been active in bringing Baha'is into the Soviet Union, the Universal House of Justice wanted to keep up with what was going on, so they asked me to come to Israel on a regular basis.

Driving around one day, I picked up a hitchhiker, a young girl in cut-offs and tank top with an Uzi strapped over her shoulder. Everyone, including women, has to serve in the Israeli army. On active duty, everyone must carry their Uzis at all times. So she showed me her Uzi. Interesting.

I made some inquiries and found there was an AA meeting in downtown Haifa. A local took me to it. It was being held in a fallout shelter right off the street. We went down into the cellar and attended the meeting.

Jerusalem is a fascinating city. The old town is thousands of years old. I went there many times while working for the Baha'i faith, and twice on Baha'i pilgrimage. Every major religion has pilgrimage as part of its practice. In most religions, the practice has died out, although it continues in the Muslim tradition of going on *Haj,* and in the Baha'i faith, which decrees that devotees should at least once in their lifetime visit the places where Baha'u'llah lived and died.

If you fly to Tel Aviv and go from there to Acca near the Lebanese border, you can visit the place where Baha'u'llah spent 26 years of his life in exile. It was a prison city during the Ottoman Empire and was a very foul place. Baha'u'llah was sent there to die, but due to the power of his personality, he was eventually released and allowed to move to the countryside at Baji. He lived out his remaining years in Baji and was buried there.

The full pilgrimage should include the house in Iran where he was born, but that site is no longer accessible. The government of Iran has destroyed many of the Baha'i pilgrimage places.

I had been on pilgrimage twice before I married Joan. After the wedding, we decided to go on pilgrimage together. It was a deeply spiritual experience for both of us. Local Baha'is serve as guides, and the Baha'i properties in Israel are very beautiful. Pilgrims are treated with such respect that it is hard not to be impressed. It's a nine-day pilgrimage and Joan was incredibly uplifted. At the end of the journey she said, "I cannot deny the truth of this religion anymore. I want to become Baha'i."

I was thrilled. I had never pushed her, or proselytized about the faith to her, but she is such an intellect that she had read many Baha'i books and had come to understand what she believed was the truth. There's a big difference between knowing something intellectually and experiencing it spiritually.

That was about four or five years ago, and we have had a wonderful spiritual Baha'i life ever since. In fact, I'd say she is more Baha'i than I am. She is on the local spiritual assembly in Colorado and active in Florida. We host Baha'i gatherings at our home, and everyone loves Joan. She always puts out a great spread.

**Cruises:** Finally, in my travels, I have to mention some of the fabulous trips we've taken with Don Morreale and his wife, Nancy Mangus. We went to Dubai with them in 2015, where we caught a ship that took us to Oman, then through the Strait of Hormuz and up the Red Sea to the Suez Canal.

On that cruise, we stopped at Haifa, Israel, where we showed Don and Nancy the beautiful Baha'i

Gardens. From there we went on to Athens and Istanbul, Turkey. It's an amazing city where we visited the famous Blue Mosque. Don also took us to the Pudding Shop, an old hippie restaurant he had visited back in the mid-70s on his way to India. Don's Irish friends, Neil and Ann Farrell met us in Istanbul, and we all hung out together there for a week.

Another trip we took with Don and Nancy was a cruise from Sydney, Australia to Honolulu. At the Sydney Opera House, we saw Tony Bennett give a concert. He was 85 years old but still incredible. He asked that the mic be turned off and was able to fill the auditorium with his voice alone. That cruise took us to American Samoa, Fiji and other Pacific islands.

**Barcelona and Northern Spain:** Don and I took a trip together before he and Nancy got married. This would have been in the Spring of 2003. Don called me up and said, "If you can leave right away, there is a transitioning cruise from Fort Lauderdale to Barcelona for $299."

I can't pass up a bargain, so I said, "I'm there!" It was an eleven-day crossing, and the ship was so empty they bumped us up to a balcony cabin. When we got to Barcelona, we rented a car and drove through the Pyrenees to Bilbao, to see the titanium clad Guggenheim Museum designed by Frank Geary.

Bottom line, it's a big world and I want to see it all before I die.

## Chapter 23: Meeting My Son and Closing the Circle

By one of those wonderful coincidences in life, my long lost son just happened to go on Ancestry.com at about the same time my brother's wife put in for it. "We may have found your uncle or your grandfather. It's a very close DNA connection," came the reply from Ancestry to my son. He immediately emailed my brother saying, "I am adopted and looking for my father. I think you may be my uncle or my grandfather."

My brother remembered the scandal from when it happened. Joan and I were at an art show at the Palm Beach Convention Center when my brother called and said, "Are you sitting down? I think we found your son."

You can imagine the shock. I had not thought of the boy that we had given up for adoption for 20 years or more. I had tried for a number of years after he was born to find him, but that was through Catholic Charities and they had sealed those records very tightly. I could not find anything out so I had given up and not thought of it for years. I immediately emailed my son Ed...Ed Strasser. He had been adopted by a loving couple who could not have children. He had been raised in a loving home and as a result was himself an incredibly loving person. When I talked to him, it was like talking to myself. His manner of speaking and his intonation were eerily similar. The content of the conversation was mainly about his life after the adoption, and mine for the last 52 years. I learned that he was a manager of a CVS Pharmacy, and that Lori, his wife to be, was also a loving person and had been helping him look for me for many years. When I said that I could come to upstate New York where they lived, he said. "No. We have a timeshare near you in Florida and we could come down to meet you." I realized that he was not after anything, that he had his own life, and that reconnecting with me would fill a hole in his heart. This is fairly common among adopted children.

    It was approximately two or three months after that that he came down to his timeshare in the town of Jupiter, which is probably less than a half hour away from where we live. I told him that when he got here, we could either meet at my house, or we could meet for lunch or dinner somewhere. He said he would love to see me at the house and we could work it out from there. So he came to the house in Delray Beach and as soon as I saw him and we talked for a while, I fell in love and I think he did too. We talked about *my* life mainly, the fact that I did not have children, and how this fulfilled the empty space in my heart, and of how I had the unexpected bonus of falling instantly in love in a way that I had never experienced before. I had never experienced such feelings, and as strange as it sounds, they were very real to me.

Ed was about six-foot-three. I don't know where he got the height from. He looks somewhat like me and as we talked, I could see some distinct Mahoney mannerisms. Lori was also there and, like me, Joan fell in love with the two of them. Joan had never had children, so it was a chance for her to fall in love as well. We all hit it off right away.

Ed and Lori had been together for about seven years, and they had not gotten married because Ed is a traditionalist and he wanted to give her a ring and have a proper marriage. He had just married off one daughter. His other daughter would be getting married within the next year or so down in Cabo San Lucas. I found that I had two granddaughters, and within a short period of time, my oldest granddaughter had a child, a boy. So now I had a great grandson. Instant family.

The first week they came down to stay in their timeshare, I realized that he had not asked Lori to marry him because of money and time. They both worked very hard. She worked in a hospital in finance and admittance. Lori is the most loving person I have ever met and very creative.

We went up to New York State to see them in their house east of Poughkeepsie, in a small town by the Connecticut border. They had just bought the house some months before. It was in a beautiful wooded area on 6 ½ acres, but it was old and needed much work. So that was taking all their money. That plus the children. Lori had four children of her own that she brought to the marriage. They were both loving parents who spent all their money on the children.

It dawned on me that one of the main reasons Ed had not asked Lori to marry him was that he could not afford a ring. I had an old cocktail ring that I'd bought

40 years before for almost nothing. It had seven beautiful diamonds, the largest being a half carat. I never wore the ring so I consulted with Joan, and we decided to give him the ring if it would help him make an honest woman out of her. So on the sixth day we were together I gave him this ring and he refused, absolutely refused, could not take it. We had just met each other and I really forced it on him. I insisted that it meant nothing to me but if it would help him, I would be happy and honored to give it to him. And so, after some persuasion, he accepted the ring. I said, "Don't tell Lori. Just have it made into a wedding band." And so he did. Within a month, he found a jeweler who designed a wedding ring from this cocktail ring. He called and said, "I did it. I got the ring and I'm gonna ask her to marry me."

    A month later, we made arrangements and got tickets to go up and see them for the surprise. We went up to his house and he had a party with her mother, all the children, and some friends of their children, and Lori and Joan and I, and he sprang this on her. He got down on one knee and asked her to marry him. It was an incredible surprise for her in a warm and loving setting with everyone there.

    Everyone pushed him to come up with a date and they said, "No we have too many obligations before we can get married," which included the fact that his second oldest daughter was planning to be married in Cabo San Lucas.

    About a year went by. We talked many times, and in one of the conversations, we set a date for the wedding. Lori got on the phone and said, "Could you perform the ceremony? You have made it possible for us to marry so we would like you to perform the ceremony."

I was shocked, humbled, and honored to be asked. I had told him that I used to perform wedding ceremonies when I first got sober in the early '80s. So when he asked me, naturally I said yes. We set the date for June 8th, 2019.

This whole experience of meeting my son is bringing some closure to my life. It's also bringing up feelings I never thought I would experience. I had decided that I wouldn't have children and I thought that was fine. I mean, as long as I had good friends and good lovers I was okay. Then I got married and realized what a wonderful thing *that* was. And then I found my son and discovered feelings that I never thought I would have. I finally came to see for myself what I'd always heard; that it's a different kind of love that you have for children. Even though he is a 52-year-old man, I still have those feelings. He's my son.

I think there was a hole in his heart too. He had met his mother some six or eight years before. She was in her 50s or early 60s. She had cancer and after the second time they met, she died of it, which was very sad for him. She had never remarried and was working as a librarian. I had lost touch with her. I knew she was adopted by a German-American family by the name of Lugar. It turns out Ed was also adopted by a German family, Strasser, which is an interesting side note.

I think my son's future is very bright. He has even talked about moving to South Florida. CVS pharmacy has many outlets near us in Palm Beach, and he is talking about seeing if he can transfer down there. Lori loves us and loves the idea of being close-by. I don't know if that will happen, but it's pretty exciting.

Who knows the future, but I believe that we will continue to have a close relationship, see each other as often as possible, and just do things together.

Now that Joan's retired, we have all the time in the world, so we could go up to see them, maybe take cruises together. We'll see how it plays out, but both of us want a true relationship with them.

His two daughters are 30 and 24, and both are married. His other children range from 22 down to 10. I got to know the 10-year-old and he's just a great kid. It's a small house they live in and with four kids in and out, plus a grandchild, it's pretty hectic. But they are such a loving family that it's nice to be around them. Nobody knows the future but I think that we will continue to have a close relationship.

# Epilogue

Working on this autobiography, I'm almost sorry that it's ending. It's been a revelation to reminisce and to see what an interesting life I've led. Looking ahead, I see the future as kind of a wonderful thing as long as I don't get full-blown Alzheimer's. I'm fighting very hard not to, and the researchers are coming out with more and more drugs to help. So I'm relying on science and hoping to stave off the symptoms as I enter my final years. There's no reason I shouldn't live into my 90s. I manage to stay happy. People say there are not enough hours in the day. I say there are exactly the right amount; 12 hours to sleep, 4 to 6 hours to lie down, and 4 to 6 hours to relax.

I've been thinking lately about what my life's greatest accomplishment has been. I'd like to say it was getting sober, but honestly, I can't take credit for that. That was God's doing, not mine.

So I think maybe my greatest accomplishment was my real estate career. Over the course of my working life, I bought, renovated, and sold something like 226 separate properties. Among all of those transactions, I've really done everything: tore down derelict buildings and replaced them with luxury townhomes, renovated single-family houses, took buildings that were just shells and turned them into affordable housing for low-income people, converted burned-out shells into high-end lofts. You name it, I've done it.

When I say I "built" these buildings, what I really mean to say is that I hired people to do the work for me. I'm neither an architect nor a contractor, although I *am* a licensed real estate agent, and I've used that particular ticket mainly to save myself a few bucks. My real estate career has been satisfying, and I couldn't have accomplished all that I did without a real passion for it. What would I do differently if I had a chance to do it all over again? Absolutely nothing! I really have no regrets.

In my remaining years (and I should live well into my 90s if Alzheimer's doesn't kill me first), I look forward to growing old and accomplishing *absolutely nothing*!!! Except maybe to grow spiritually, which would be a tremendous accomplishment in and of itself.

Oddly enough, I don't have – and really never have had – a burning desire to succeed. I have a lazy brain, and so far it has served me well. These days I average ten to eleven hours of sleep per night. I very seldom get angry. I'm blessed insofar as I have made enough money to enjoy my old age. And best of all, I married a wonderful woman to spend my remaining years with.

When I die, I want to be buried according to the dictates of my Baha'i faith, which states that we should be interred within 24 hours of *when* we die, and within an hour's travel of *where* we die. Of course, this law was made in the days before refrigeration and embalming, but it is still adhered to by Baha'is. So, if possible, that would be my preference.

I suppose I'd like to be remembered as a spiritual human being who tried his best, even given my propensity towards laziness. I really don't look forward to the end, but I really am not worried too much about it. No matter how I die, I believe it will be God's plan, and I'm okay with that.

When I took care of my father for the five years before he died of Alzheimer's, I watched his steady decline. Within a month of his impending death, there was no vocabulary left, no eye contact, nothing. He just shuffled around as the disease crawled deeper into his brain, and he became increasingly frail. But I'll never forget watching him in his bedroom as he would get down on his knees and mumble something incoherent. I had to assume he was praying. That told me that there is something about us human beings that is essentially spiritual, and that that essential core in each of us does not die.

As for the next generation, I never really thought much about them because I myself had no children. And then I met my son, and all of a sudden, I had a genetic family, which has really affected my view of life, and of how we humans are ruining the planet and killing ourselves. While I don't believe that I myself will see the end of life on this planet, I do believe that we no longer have any real chance of preventing it. So we'd better get the hell off the planet before it's too late.

This may sound far-fetched, but there is news every day of how new people are getting into the outer space business. Elon Musk, for example, just sent the first Tesla into space. So I think there is hope for the survival of the human species… just not here on earth. I see it as a race between the engineering that is killing us and the engineering that will save us. So I'm hoping with a new fervor that the human race will have a glorious future on some other planet. My prejudice is this; that if we do meet aliens in outer space, we will be at the top of the heap. Probably not, but I can always hope.

*The End*

Made in the USA
Middletown, DE
13 July 2019